ATLA Monograph Series
edited by Dr. Kenneth E. Rowe

12. Thomas Virgil Peterson. *Ham and Japheth: The Mythic World of Whites in the Antebellum South.* 1978.
13. Randall K. Burkett. *Garveyism as a Religious Movement: The Institutionalization of a Black Civil Religion.* 1978.
14. Roger G. Betsworth. *The Radical Movement of the 1960's.* 1980.
15. Alice Cowan Cochran. *Miners, Merchants, and Missionaries: The Roles of Missionaries and Pioneer Churches in the Colorado Gold Rush and Its Aftermath, 1858-1870.* 1980.
16. Irene Lawrence. *Linguistics and Theology: The Significance of Noam Chomsky for Theological Construction.* 1980.
17. Richard E. Williams. *Called and Chosen: The Story of Mother Rebecca Jackson and the Philadelphia Shakers.* 1981.
18. Arthur C. Repp, Sr. *Luther's Catechism Comes to America: Theological Effects on the Issues of the Small Catechism Prepared In or For America Prior to 1850.* 1982.
19. Lewis V. Baldwin. *"Invisible" Strands in African Methodism.* 1983.
20. David W. Gill. *The Word of God in the Ethics of Jacques Ellul.* 1984.
21. Robert Booth Fowler. *Religion and Politics in America.* 1985.
22. Page Putnam Miller. *A Claim to New Roles.* 1985.
23. C. Howard Smith. *Scandinavian Hymnody from the Reformation to the Present.* 1987.
24. Bernard T. Adeney. *Just War, Political Realism, and Faith.* 1988.

JUST WAR, POLITICAL REALISM, AND FAITH

by

Bernard T. Adeney

ATLA Monograph Series, No. 24

The American Theological Library Association
and
The Scarecrow Press, Inc.
Metuchen, N.J., & London
1988

Library of Congress Cataloging-in-Publication Data

Adeney, Bernard T., 1948-
  Just war, political realism, and faith/by Bernard T. Adeney.
    p. cm. — (ATLA monograph series ; no. 24)
  Bibliography: p.
  Includes index.
  ISBN 0-8108-2152-4
  1. Nuclear warfare—Religious aspects—Christianity.
2. Nuclear warfare—Moral and ethical aspects. 3. Just war
doctrine. 4. War—Religious aspects—Christianity.
5. War—Moral and ethical aspects. I. American Theological
Library Association. II. Title. III. Series.
BR115.A85A34 1988
241'.6242—dc19   88-16605

TO

FRANCES SCRENOCK ADENEY

TABLE OF CONTENTS

EDITOR'S FOREWORD

Since 1972 the American Theological Library Association, through its standing committee on publication, has undertaken responsibility for a modest monograph series in the field of religious studies. Our aim in this series is to publish two dissertations of quality each year at reasonable cost. Titles are selected from studies in a wide range of religious and theological disciplines. We are pleased to publish Bernard T. Adeney's study of "just war" as number twenty-four in our series.

Bernard Temple Adeney took his undergraduate degree at the University of Wisconsin where he graduated with honors in English and Asian studies. Mr. Adeney studied abroad, first at the Alliance Française in Paris, then at the Discipleship Training Center in Singapore, and finally at the University of London where he received the B.D. degree. In 1982 he received the doctorate in the religion and society program of the Graduate Theological Union in Berkeley. Author of numerous scholarly articles, Mr. Adeney is currently Assistant Professor of Social Ethics in the New College for Advanced Christian Studies in Berkeley, California.

Kenneth E. Rowe
Series Editor
Drew University Library
Madison, NJ 07940

PREFACE

I am in debt to many people for the completion of this work. I benefited greatly from the critical input of John C. Bennet, Robert McAfee Brown, Ernst B. Haas and William B. Spohn, S.J.. They continually encouraged me to hone my thinking and my argument to a sharper edge. They, and I, know that my struggle with the issues in this book is not completed.

Thanks are also due to the community of people of whom I am a part. The practical encouragement of my parents and of friends in the "Ark" made the burden of writing lighter. Special thanks are due to Mary Phillips and Robert Welch who typed successive drafts and helped with the editing. My colleagues at New College Berkeley, Bill Dyrness, David Gill and Joel Green, helpfully prodded me to complete the final draft.

My family has deeply shared the creative struggle that went into this work. I am grateful to Jennifer, Rina and Peter for their sustaining love, creative encouragement at the end of each chapter, and boundless hope in the significance of my writing.

My deepest gratitude is to my wife, Fran, who has been a growing friend, fearless critic, a partner in thought and life, and a fellow disciple on the road. This book would not have been possible had it not been for her deep love and support over the past twenty years.

INTRODUCTION

Modern technology, especially nuclear weaponry, has expanded the problems of conflict in international relations. Changes in politics and technology may require us to change the fundamental way we think about war. This book examines the nature of modern war in relation to two prominent traditions of thought about war: just war theory and political realism. Just war theory dominates as a tradition through which Christians have subjected war to ethical and theological analysis. Both as a mode of thinking and as a set of principles, just war theory frames an understanding of war through the questions it asks. This work evaluates how well the tradition of justifiable war addresses the problems of modern war.

Political realism discounts moral questions posed by just war theory and explains war without reference to ethics. It also frames a normative picture of reality through the metaphors it uses. We will consider how well political realism explains international political behavior and how adequate are the normative assumptions on which it is based.

In chapter one we set the problem by examining how warfare has changed over the past two hundred years. Political changes have transformed the way war is fought. The French Revolution and the rise of nationalism made war the business of whole societies rather than the exclusive province of a military elite. The accelerating growth of military technology increased civilian participation in war, making it possible to attack an enemy's will by striking its populations.

Technology has increased the abstraction involved in battle as war became a competition between technologies. Technology has also changed the nature of peace. The military profession has been diffused into more and more sectors of society as the arms race has become routinized as a permanent function of government.

The pinnacle of technological achievement in warfare is nuclear weapons. The thermonuclear bomb forced a major change in our perception of both war and peace. Nuclear weapons are a permanent part of our culture and force us to reexamine the meaning of our future.

Chapter two examines how Christian ethics examined war in the past by developing just war theory. Although just war theory is not necessarily the best vehicle for the moral evaluation of war, it merits close analysis because of its enormous influence on Christian thinking about war. Most great figures in the intellectual history of the Church wrote about war from within this tradition.

Four different kinds of just war theory emerge prior to the twentieth century. The writings of the Roman political philosopher, Cicero, represent the first of these "stages." Cicero's theory turned both on "natural reason" and the spread of natural reason. According to Cicero, Roman law and government most closely approximated natural law. Therefore the good of the world required the acceptance of Roman rule. Just war theory thus became a strategy for empire.

In the second stage, Augustine approached the problem of war by facing the painful conflict between Christian love and requirements of national defense. The tension of this conflict engendered a mode of moral reasoning about war that sought to do justice to both sides of the issue. Augustine's solution separated the absolute ethic of the Christian individual from the relative moral requirements of the state. Augustine believed that political necessity required a political ruler to fight just wars with an internal motivation of love.

In the Middle Ages just war theory drew from Augustine an elaborate set of rules designed to limit the justifiable occasions of war and restrict the permissible means of warfare. These rules provide the basis of most subsequent discussion of just war theory.

The fourth stage of just war theory tabled the moral question of just war and sought practical means to limit the brutality of its conduct. Secularized just war theory was based on social contract theory and developed rules of warfare based on reciprocal self-interest. This form of the theory gave birth to modern international law.

Chapter three considers the changes in the nature of war introduced by nuclear weapons. War with nuclear weapons is no longer a contest of military strength but a bargaining process based on the manipulation of risk. The physical power of nuclear weapons is beyond imagination and has forced a revolution in military strategy. Clearly rational choices are not present among the available strategic options for nuclear defense. This dilemma raises urgent questions about the relation between rationality and morality in nuclear policy.

Chapter four examines modern just war theory. As an abstract mode of reasoning just war theory has a permanent validity. It is a validity which tries to find minimally acceptable ways to restrict international conflict. Just war theory seeks to reconcile the need for national defense with defense of the innocent in war.

As a concrete set of rules, just war theory is anachronistic because it fails to address the unique problems of deterrence in a nuclear age. The fundamental problem with just war theory is the impossibility of effectively defending a nation in modern war without breaking the canons of just warfare. A second area of difficulty is the ineffectiveness of the principle of discrimination as a means for the protection of the innocent. The key moral problem of modern war is the strategy of deterrence. None of the attempts to reconcile deterrence with just war theory has succeeded.

If the traditional moral attempts to grasp the problem of modern war have failed, is morality irrelevant to modern war? In chapter five we examine political realism as an attempt to explain international conflict without making normative assumptions. After a brief survey of the history of realist thought, we look at the structural theory of one prominent modern realist.

Classical political realism proposes a set of metaphors and concepts but forms an ideal type of international politics. This ideal type powerfully demonstrates pressures that exist in international relations. But realism's claim to objective, amoral analysis is faulty because the facts selected for interpretation provide a restricted and value-laden view of the world.

The failure of both just war theory and political realism to deal with the moral issues of nuclear war lead to an analysis in the final chapter of how Christian ethics can face both the moral issue and the political problem of nuclear weapons. I suggest that the central question must be how we can lessen the criminal burden of the possession of nuclear weapons.

There is an acute tension between the moral commitments of Christian discipleship and the necessities of governmental politics. Many forms of ethical dualism have been suggested in the past but none completely satisfy the need. I suggest ethical analysis that addresses both "horns" of the dilemma in two linked but separate approaches. Christian ethics require that the problem of nuclear weapons be realistically addressed at the level of policy. At the same time, the values of the Kingdom of God call for vigorous unqualified protest against the evil that nuclear weapons represent.

CHAPTER 1

THE PROBLEM OF WAR IN
THE MODERN WORLD

The meaning of war has changed significantly in the last two centuries. Some change resulted from accelerating technology; some from political changes associated with the development of the modern nation-state. Nuclear weapons represent the most dramatic change in war. But even apart from nuclear weapons, the meaning of war has changed.

First we trace the political and social changes in war introduced by the French Revolution.

Second we examine how the rapid growth in technology further changed warfare by making non-combatant populations vulnerable on a new scale to military attack.

The third section examines the reciprocal influences of technology, politics and culture.

In the fourth section we consider the effects of modern war on peaceful society and the nature of peace.

The last section of this chapter considers, in social terms, the meaning of nuclear weapons.

Napoleon and the Development of Mass Warfare

Perhaps the most significant political change in the nature of warfare resulted from the rise of nationalism. In the eighteenth century, the mitigation of the cruelty of warfare made considerable strides forward. The end of the wars of religion and the dawn of the Enlightenment brought great hopes for universal peace. Warfare was highly formalized and professionalized. A cosmopolitan spirit prevailed in Europe. The rise in republicanism and capitalism indicated a probable rejection of the aristocratic interest in war.

Warfare displayed mildness during the Enlightenment partially because the practice was an aristocratic concern. Warfare was a game between gentlemen. The troops were mercenaries disinterested in losing their lives for any cause. The common soldier was usually pressed into the army from the poorest and least productive segments of society. He required extensive training and brutal control to force him to act in prescribed patterns and not desert.

A sharp distinction was drawn between the military and non-military elements of society. In the interest of preserving the valuable productive capabilities of a country, statesmen recruited their armies from non-productive segments of the population: officers from the nobility and soldiers from the unemployed, the dissatisfied, the criminals, etc. The growing middle-class generated the wealth necessary to support armies without looting or pillaging. Rigorous and often brutal discipline of the troop was necessary to maintain control.

Because of the use of artillery and armies in mass formation, bloody battles were common. However, the carnage was often avoided as each side attempted to wear out the other with elaborate maneuvers. Daniel Defoe said that

> ... in his day it was customary for armies of fifty thousand men to spend the whole campaign in dodging each other. The art of war was said by another to consist less in knowing how to defend a fortress than in knowing how to surrender it honorably.[1]

A remarkable aspect of war at this time was the lack of hatred. Soldiers were not involved in the issues over which war was fought. Most armies were composed of mercenaries from various nations. Generals often left the service of one sovereign in order to serve under another. As much as possible civilians were excluded from the effects of war. Frederick the Great remarked that when he was engaged in war, the civilian population should not even know a war was taking place.[2]

The French Revolution dramatically changed the way war was fought. Nationalism encouraged large masses of people to become politically motivated, and the passion generated by mass patriotism was organized on behalf of a military cause. With the call to liberate the whole world on behalf of "liberty, equality and fraternity," the professional detachment of 18th century was lost. War became, not a contest between two armies or monarchs, but a life and death struggle between whole societies.

Mass warfare was not in itself a new element in the history of war. War has been "total" many times before. What was new was a quantum jump in the scale and organization of war. Part of this change in scale was the result of a changed concept of political sovereignty. Kings had been responsible for the common defense and honor. They were contractors who employed others to fight wars. As the monarchy was overthrown and the people became theoretically sovereign, the issue of war as well as its conduct became everyone's concern. The "professionalism" of the army broke down and instead of a rigidly stratified social organization, the army became an instrument of democracy.

This change did not come easily or smoothly. The beginnings of the democratization of the French army were chaotic. Many trained officers emigrated and total defeat was staved off only because other nations continued to fight by eighteenth century rules of chivalry. According to Hoffman Nickerson, war was considered, "... a game played for prizes and not for the political life and death of states and peoples, a thing of skill rather than brute force."[3]

Napoleon's organizational genius made the new French army a formidable force. His skill did not lie in the classical art of intricate battlefield maneuvers. Rather Napoleon knew how to raise, motivate and move large numbers of soldiers from one point to another where they would be thrown directly into battle.

Soldiers were no longer a professional trained and disciplined force, but a highly motivated mass of individuals out to change the world.

> No longer was it necessary, for authority with the help of the cudgel, to suppress the self-preserving reactions of the soldier by reconditioning his normal reflexes. These reactions were now suppressed in consequence of the soldier's identification with a larger self...[4]

This larger "self" was embodied first in the Revolution,

then in France and finally in Napoleon.

Systematic propaganda became crucial to the war effort at an unprecedented scale. As large numbers of highly motivated patriots could be raised with relative ease, the tactics of warfare underwent a dramatic transformation.

> The tactics of the eighteenth century armies were limited by the necessity of keeping at least the infantry in strict formation, for only in these formations could the soldier behave as was expected of him—like an automaton. In contrast, the strongly motivated French soldier could be allowed considerable freedom.[5]

The most significant change in tactics was in proportionality. Not only were non-combatants drawn into the struggle, but the lives of soldiers became of little value. The French soldier was not the product of years of training and could be replaced with relatively little effort. Bonaparte threw large numbers of troops directly into battle and replaced them when they were slaughtered. "Democracy had made men cheap."[6]

A changing view of the acceptable costs of warfare also affected the whole of society as it was drawn into war. A vivid illustration of this is the following excerpt from a law passed in 1793 by the French National convention to assure "the permanent requisition of all Frenchmen for the defense of the country."

> The young men shall fight, the married men shall forge weapons and transport supplies; the women will make tents and clothes and serve in the hospitals; the children will make up old linen into lint; the old men will have themselves carried into the public squares to rouse the courage of the fighting men, to preach hatred against kings and the unity of the republic.[7]

Nationalism introduced a new concept of war. The nineteenth century Prussian soldier, Carl Von Clausewitz, understood this and predicted that

> ... henceforth war would involve not merely a small segment of specialists, tending to lapse into mediocrity,

their intellectual horizons circumscribed by an ossified doctrine. War was now democratized. It became everybody's business, and the art of war could be nurtured by the resources of the entire nation.[8]

The Napoleonic wars introduced a new kind of warfare to Europe and in the process fed the rising nationalism. The patriotic feelings of other nations were roused by the slaughter and they too adopted the politics of mass warfare necessary to defeat Napoleon.

Clausewitz understood the important changes brought about by the French Revolution. Yet his categories defining violence in warfare reveal an inability to foresee the further changes technology would bring. The twentieth century explosion of technology produced a new kind of warfare based on the resources of entire societies. Ideology and democracy laid the burden of warfare on everyone. The growth of an industrial society made it possible in a new way for everyone to be involved in the war effort.

The Growing Influence of Technology on the Nature of War

The most significant leap in military technology since the invention of the steamship was the development of air power. In a celebrated essay, Edward Meade Earle commented on the link between air power and other technologies:

The development of military aviation... has been in-separably related to collateral advances in metallurgy, physics, automotive transport, photography, wireless telegraphy, automatic weapons, electronics, and the whole vast complex of scientific and industrial research and techniques.[9]

Air power did more than give the military a more destructive and maneuverable weapon. Air power made it possible to attack the capacity and will of one's enemies before defeating their military forces. The use of an air force "advanced" the involvement of whole societies from participating in the sustenance of warfare to involvement also as a major target of war. To the traditional meaning of military power as the physical defence of a country, was added the need to prevent the enemy from using its power against one's own population.

According to Earle, this had two major consequences for the nature of war.[10] Firstly,

> ... it changes the political relationships between states so drastically as to put the peacefully inclined and the militarily careless at a heavy initial disadvantage in any war of survival.

Secondly, cities become a direct target in war.

> No amount of nostalgia can blink the stubborn fact than an industrial society will fight wars which are battles of production and logistics—contests between production lines and mechanized communication.

The capacity to fight a war lay in the state's industry, primarily located in its cities. Military and industrial transportation as well as political administration flow out from the city.

> No nation possessed of sea power has ever abandoned the blockade; it is unlikely that any nation possessed of air power will abandon bombing as a means of immobilizing the enemy.[11]

One response to the increasing destructiveness of war technology was the hope that

> ... war has now at last become so awesome that no thinking man could possibly take the risk of involving his people in a new conflict. Pacifists thought they saw the handwriting on the wall when balloons soared into the sky, carrying the possibility of a new and overwhelming front against armies, military bases and cities. In turn, the airplane, long range artillery, and especially poison gas seemed to hold the key to frightening men into a better world.[12]

Unfortunately, none of these inventions prevented war for long. What they did do was steadily increase the destructive potential of war. More significantly technological innovation provided the means for making civilians the targets of war. Nationalism brought the common people into the fervor and instigation of war. Technology made it possible for them to become its victims.

Technology has also changed the nature of killing in warfare. It has often been noted that the growth of war technology has heightened impersonality. This impersonality is not only a product of the distance and detachment technology makes possible, it is also a result of the complexity of any conflict between technologically sophisticated societies. When one person kills another it is a simple and immediate act, whether done with a laser or a knife. When whole societies wield enormous power against each other, the complexity involved heightens abstraction.

Technological society is dependent upon the use of abstract symbols. The more complex the power that is wielded, the more abstract become the symbols. This is true of all modern professions.

> A banker or stock market tycoon may never see more money than is in his pocket, likewise a military commander-in-chief can sustain a successful career without ever seeing a corpse.[13]

Modern warfare is not only between people and states, but also between technologies. What must be defended and attacked is not just military personnel but also missiles, airports, communication systems, factories, transportation systems, power stations, research facilities, satellites, harbors, etc.. Human beings become more and more incidental to the technologies which they operate. "Collateral" damage often refers to people killed incidental to the destruction of a target.

The abstract quality of modern war is further enhanced by the diffusion of the war effort. Complexity demands a division of labor and responsibility. Institutional and bureaucratic imperatives often determine a course of action without reference to the final goal of the activity. The incredible amount of cooperative and coordinated activity spreads the responsibility for action so widely that it may be felt by no one. The worker who helps manufacture microchips which will eventually help guide a missile may have little concept of the final results of the use of that product. Military activities are often divorced from the violence they serve. As Rapoport says,

> The accessory activities of war have become so dominant that their end result recedes beyond the horizon of imagination. The vast bulk of war activity today is production, planning, organization, communication, logistic calculations of capabilities, etc. etc.[14]

Part of the abstractness of modern warfare is inherent in the technologies themselves which place vast distances between opponents. One dying person before ones eyes has more emotional impact than the news of a thousand dead many miles away. As the destructiveness of technology increases, such abstraction becomes a psychological necessity. We shy away from understanding the suffering of even our nearest neighbors. Grappling with suffering caused by megatechnological warfare is beyond the limits of human sanity.[15] We abstract warfare into numbers and concepts accessible to limited definition. Thus, we protect ourselves from going mad.

The Power of Technology

The popular myth that science and technology are the primary hope for humanity is rivaled today by the equally powerful myth that technology is the primary cause of the greatest human problems. Both myths share the assumption that human meaning and value are intimately linked to material culture and environment. The positive view suggests that while science and technology may create problems for society, they provide the most significant tools for the solution of those problems. Technology is seen as an extension of human power through which people can control their environment and shape it to meet their needs.

> The negative perspective suggests that the opposite is in fact the case. Technology is not the tool but the master. Human culture can be the servant of technological culture. Technology has its own momentum and shapes human culture to its own ends.[16]

These opposing myths may both have a core of truth to them, yet neither adequately accounts for the role of technology in human culture. A synthesis of elements from both myths helps but gives answers before the questions are accurately defined. Both the problems and the solutions of technology are coherent in the context of a normative structure that proposes a meaning to human history and culture. It is my assumption that technology is not a "neutral" factor that may be used or ignored according to human will.

Hegel believed that the idea of a civilization determined its basic institutions and that this idea developed technologies to realize itself. From this perspective, technology is not "neutral" because it incorporates the values of those who create it.

Marx reversed this line of thinking by suggesting that technology shaped the economy which in turn determined the major structures of society. According to him, the religious, political, moral and ideological super-structures of society could ultimately be traced, through economics, to technology. The viewpoint of Marx gives precedence to material factors in the shaping of institutions and values. In contrast, Hegel understood mind or ideas as the impetus for the shaping of our material environment with technology.

Both of these perspectives are helpful tools for understanding technology. However, one cannot be chosen over the other as dominant. Technology both shapes human culture and is shaped by it. Quincy Wright puts it this way:

> Technology is an integral aspect of culture. The group's culture, both moral and material, influence its capacity to invent and to utilize technological innovations and the introduction of technological innovations will effect

changes in the entire culture.[17]

Technology is cumulative and irreversible.[18] While it would be unwise to say that technology can never be lost or suppressed, history suggests that the reversal of technological "progress" is extremely rare. Even after the apparent total destruction of Germany and Japan's industrial incapacity following World War II, those countries very swiftly regained and surpassed their former level of technology.

This should lend caution to those who place their hope in the elimination of nuclear weapons. Apart from a short period of time in the eighteenth century, there is very little evidence that weapons technology has ever been suppressed for political or moral reasons. In spite of periodic, vigorous protests about the increasing barbarity of warfare, no weapons technology, once tried, has ever been dismantled. In the twelfth century, a humanitarian pope threatened to excommunicate anyone who would use that cruel and barbaric new invention, the crossbow. What was once barbaric soon becomes accepted. Even napalm may appear humane in comparison to nuclear fallout. Today the atom bomb that razed Hiroshima is considered "small" in comparison to thermonuclear devices.

One response to the apparent irreversibility of technological innovation is the insistence that the present situation of the world is quite different from that of the past. Weapons technology today threatens human survival. It is dangerous to extrapolate from the past to the future concerning the relationship of humans to technology. The future is both unique and mysterious. Nevertheless, the prospects for the elimination of modern weapons technology appear bleak at best. Necessity does not automatically create possibility.

Anatol Rapoport observed that there is no correlation between the "success" of a culture and the "success" of its technology. An example is the coincidence of the invention of gunpowder with the decline of feudalism in the late middle ages. With the introduction of artillery, according to Rapoport,

... the walled castle ceased to give protection to the feudal lords and their serfs and so ceased to perpetuate the loyalty of the serfs to the lords. Thus an innovation that 'succeeded', that was accepted and reproduced, led to the demise of the culture in which it became embedded.[19]

The irreversibility of technology does not imply that there is "no hope" of controlling the use of nuclear weapons. Nor should the concern for arms control and disarmament be minimized. But the first step in coming to grips with the reality of modern war technology is to recognize that it is a fact that will not go away. A World Council of Churches document says,

We now possess nuclear weapons, we shall always possess the knowledge of how to produce them. They have become a permanent aspect of human culture.[20]

The reciprocal influence of politics and technology on each other would be difficult to overestimate. The growth of technology is directly related to the perceived political needs of a culture. Politics and technology interact dialectically. As change occurs it is often impossible to determine which is cause and which is effect. The enormous growth of the nation-state since the French Revolution has provided a channel for the development and control of technology.

The unprecedented planning and contracting capabilities of the modern state have enabled technology to develop at a rapid pace to meet political needs. The putative defense requirements of the state have been the single greatest impetus for technological innovation. The state is able to marshal vast amounts of material and intellectual resources and bring them to bear on the extension of its military technology. This produces breakthroughs not only in weaponry but also in communications, transportation, electronics, photography, chemistry, etc..

While the state has influenced both the direction and the scope of technological innovation, technology has transformed the scope and function of the state. A major purpose of the state technologies. The control of military power which may not be wielded by the private individual is an obvious example. In the technologies of mass communication, transportation, medicine, education and industry, the state exercises control and has thereby greatly increased its power and purpose. With the growth of the state has come a corresponding growth in the effect of defense policy on national life.

Changes in Warfare and the Nature of Peace

Changes in war through technological and political "growth" have increasingly affected peacetime society. The incredibly destructive potential of modern military technology has created a fear, not only of other nations but of war itself. For the first time in history, the race to build up military power is motivated as much by the desire to prevent war as to win it. Security has always been a high priority for states. Defense policy is now dominating national priorities in peace-time as never before.

In 1941, Harold Lasswell predicted that a state's perception of, and response to modern international insecurity would have a profound effect on the internal organization of its society. Lasswell's "garrison state hypothesis" suggested that if the following two conditions dominated international relations, the effects on internal societies would be profound.

1.) The power elites value power enough to resort to large scale coercion when they regard such coercive strategies as useful to the maintenance of their ascendancy;

2.) The elites accept the expectation that the retention of power...depends upon capability and willingness to coerce internal or external challengers.[21]

Lasswell predicted that if the above conditions combined with modern military technology, the insecurity of a "garrisoned world" would undermine democracy and encourage totalitarianism. Political and economic values would be subordinated to increased military power. Thus Lasswell observed,

Perpetual apprehension of war keeps the accent upon
consideration of power measured as fighting potential...
(and) the appraisal of all social values and institutional
practices with state power considerations in view.
Economic values and institutions are drawn into
preparation of weapons and thereby subordinated to
power... Family and ecclesiastical institutions are given
encouragement so long as they interpose no ideological or
behavioral obstacles to national security.[22]

Lasswell's hypothesis concerning effect of international
insecurity on domestic organization is a simplified "ideal
type" of political behavior. But the basic cogency of his
hypothesis is well supported by the economic priorities of the
Reagan Administration. All governmental programs are
considered potentially expendable unless they relate to
defense policy. If the pressing strategic question is how do we
prevent our "enemies" from using their weapons on our
population, an accompanying ethical question must be what do
we become in our search for security.

Initially, the democratization of war detracted from the
professionalism that characterized eighteenth century war. In
the twentieth century, to prepare and wage war has become
professional as well as democratic. Modern war technology is
not confined to a single segment of society easily isolated or
controlled by the rest of society. As Rapoport observed,

The grumblings against the "military-industrial" complex
in the U.S. today are not likely to rise above the level of
rhetoric, because the "complex" is not a profession whose
activity one could regulate, circumscribe, or altogether
prohibit.[23]

Estimates suggest that up to 50% of scientific research in
the United States today is related in some way to security
needs. One result of this high percentage is that the war
profession serves the career needs of not only the military but
of a large cross-section of society.

The diffusion of the war profession tends to reinforce the
values that produced it. Those who have a vested interest in
security-related professions are not likely to attack the values

which support their own interests. Political and military interests tend to be mutually reinforcing. There is hardly a congressional district in the United States that does not have some kind of military installation on it that provides jobs for the populace. Even congressional representatives who favor cuts in the military budget are not anxious to see projects in their own districts cut back. Thus, a mutually reinforcing dynamic is set up through which military values are encouraged by civilian economic interests and economic interests are supported by an institutionalized arms race.

"Arms racing" is not a new phenomenon. Throughout history one of the greatest stimulations to technological innovation has been the desire to find a new weapon or a new technique which would give one's nation power over the enemy. Fear that the enemy might find a technological path to dominance spurs the process. A major portion of arms racing in the past dealt with the costly process of mobilizing for war. The task of raising revenues, manufacturing weapons, calling up an army and training it was a complex process by which the state focused its resources on achieving a peak of readiness, before an enemy could strike first.

Arms races of this type are primarily competitions to achieve a quantitative superiority. Once such a race is undertaken war becomes extremely likely. The peak of preparedness cannot be maintained indefinitely and the longer it is maintained the greater chance the enemy has of "catching up." Any relaxation might lose the advantage gained. Arms races were preparations with the assumption of imminent war. Few quantitative arms races in history have not led to war.

Amazement has been expressed that the arms race between the Soviet Union and the United States has lasted forty years without resulting in a direct war between the two. The standard explanation for this unique phenomenon is that nuclear weapons have created a deterrent to war that amounts to a stalemate. Yet the arms race must continue because neither can trust that the other side will not find the means of breaking the deadlock with some new innovation.

The essential feature of the Soviet-American arms race is the competition for qualitative breakthroughs. Of course the quantitative arms race continues but is over-shadowed by the race for technological superiority. A sense of security can never be found based on numbers alone because the real danger is that the opponent may achieve a technological breakthrough that would nullify the "balance" between the two. A qualitative arms race can never reach a "peak" of preparedness because there is no theoretical limit to technological inventiveness.

The arms race is as much a race against the frontiers of science and technology as it is a competition with another state. Because the competition is not focused upon an imminently expected real war, the goals of the competition are abstract. The focus is on destructive potential, capabilities and worst possible scenarios. Because there is no foreseeable end to the arms race, it becomes institutionalized. Arms racing is no longer an unusual sprint towards superiority but a normal routinized part of government.

Some political scientists have questioned whether there even is an arms race between the United States and the Soviet Union.

Albert Wohlstetter argues that the term "arms race" is misleading. The build-up in arms between the Soviet Union and the United States has not been a result of each side responding to the other but reflects the routinized build-up of power in response to many different requirements of the modern state.[24] Congressman Les Aspin (D.Wis.) published a series of charts comparing the Soviet arms build-up with that of Germany before World War II.[25] Germany had a dramatic and swift build-up in a short time whereas the Soviet Union has maintained a fairly steady build-up over a long period. While no firm conclusions can be drawn from the study, it reinforces the impression of the routinized, institutionalized character of the arms race.

The arms race is both limited by economic factors and promoted by special economic interests. Many people's careers depend on Pentagon dollars. New weapons systems justify their own inclusion in the budget and help win contracts for their proponents. The various armed services also compete with each other for a larger portion of the budget. New "provocative" technology is able to attract more congressional attention and interest than more mundane needs.

Technological momentum also influences arms building. There is a very large and influential technical community which thinks up new systems and wants to see if they will work. Defense Secretary Robert McNamara experienced heavy pressures from the technical community and said,

> There is a kind of mad momentum intrinsic to the development of all nuclear weaponry. If a system works —and works well—there is strong pressure from many directions, to produce and deploy the weapon out of all proportion to the prudent level required.[26]

What Ted Greenwood calls "the inexorable drive of bureaucratic process" also plays a part in the eventual deployment of new systems.[27] Once the huge bureaucracy of the defense establishment begins to roll in favor of a major system it is very difficult to stop. Often the Arms Control and Disarmament Agency will not even hear about a new weapons system until it is too late for effective debate.

The elaborate complexity of weapons systems results in a lead time of five to ten years from conception to production. This means that the decisions on whether or not to develop a new weapons system depends on estimates of what will be needed five to fifteen years in the future. Such thinking requires predicting the state of Soviet technology and the climate of international tensions. In the absence of reliable knowledge, it is always thought better to be on the safe side. Unfortunately conservative estimates of needs based on "worst possible case" scenarios can become self-fulfilling prophecies.

John Steinbrunner argues that the conservative planning principle has been built into the force planning calculations that structure decisions throughout the defense bureaucracy. "In the process," he says, "these assumptions have gained the enormous policy momentum which only the set routine of very large organizations can import."[28]

The current arms race is not analogous to arms races in the past. The technological society has created a process of technological innovation in the field of weapons systems that cannot be easily stopped because its causes are many and complex. Greenwood suggests that any unilateral reduction in the rate of technological weapons innovation is extremely unlikely. He says,

> The institutional incentive of the aerospace industry, the military services and D.D.R. & E. [Department of Defense Research and Engineering], to continually generate new possibilities are so powerful, the need for civilian decision makers to hedge against uncertain but possible Soviet actions are so high, changes in perceptions about strategic requirements so likely, and countervailing forces so weak that the possibility of unilateral restraint appears quite dim.[29]

Unlike the arms races of the past, the qualitative arms race of technological societies is a race against the ever receding frontiers of science. With the Strategic Defense Initiative (S.D.I.), the frontiers of defense technology have taken another quantum leap.

Although a qualitative arms race may not be as destabilizing as the quantitative races of the past, an arms race that swallows so many resources and expends so much time and energy of the technological elite, must have a profound long term effect on the society involved. The arms race diffuses military involvement throughout society and blunts the edges of all values that conflict with security.

The Meaning of Nuclear Weapons

Nuclear weapons are a permanent fact of modern life. The existence of nuclear weapons is a fact worth noting because of its relation to a pattern of meaning and values. We consider nuclear weapons noteworthy because we value their relation to actual and potential events we care about. There is never only one way to perceive a fact. The perspectives of a U.S. strategic analyst, a Swiss peasant, a Russian intellectual, a Kremlin advisor or a homeless street person will each be different. This difference is the product of varying levels of knowledge and of different value systems and perceptions of what is important. The "facticity" of nuclear weapons turns out to be many facts with many interpretations.

One nuclear physicist I spoke with perceived nuclear weapons through an analogy to hydrogen explosions on the surface of the sun. To him, nuclear weapons are technical devices through which awesome but natural amounts of nuclear explosions continually provide the energy that gives life to the world. In contrast, an anti-nuclear activist spoke of nuclear weapons as a great idol. The analogy she expressed was not of the sun but of hell. Analogies while not right or wrong, are appropriate or inappropriate in relation to their context of meaning.

The existence of nuclear weapons is an actual fact. The use of nuclear weapons in war is a potential fact. Both these facts are not merely material realities. The "costs and benefits" of nuclear weapons are psychological, social, symbolic and spiritual as well as material. The effects of nuclear weapons cannot be neatly divided into good and evil. The greatest impact of nuclear weapons, thus far, was not the apocalyptic destruction of Hiroshima and Nagasaki, but the change in human consciousness about war and the future, which Hiroshima inaugurated.

Nuclear weapons are a social reality whose meaning is partly derived from the vision one holds of society. For many people who unconditionally oppose nuclear weapons, there is no room in their vision of society for the existence of such weapons.

For others, nuclear weapons are an apt symbol of the power and potential of technological culture. While the danger of nuclear weapons is "understood," the danger is not considered insurmountable. Nuclear power symbolizes the transformation of "man into superman" through science and technology.

Still another social vision sees the United States as the major hope of preserving freedom and democracy in the world, by holding back the tide of tyranny. Nuclear weapons, in their vision symbolize American power and might in the service of truth, justice and freedom.

Increasing numbers of people perceive nuclear weapons as a confirmation of their cynicism about society. For them nuclear weapons underline the "gut feeling" that there is no future.

Meaning must be existentially experienced in the present or not at all.

In reality, most people's perception of nuclear weapons is both more complex and probably more confused than any of the above simple positions. It is difficult to come to grips with the reality of nuclear weapons. The mind shrinks from confronting a magnitude of power which is beyond comprehension. Nuclear weapons, from my perspective, should never fit comfortably into our view of society.

They are an intolerable social reality which nevertheless is a permanent part of human culture for the foreseeable future. The result is an irreducible tension.

Conclusion

The unique problems of modern war are related to an incredibly complex set of technological and political factors. Nuclear weapons are perhaps the most significant single part of this network but they are only one part.

What Clausewitz called the "art of War" has been greatly changed by both political and technological innovations. War is no longer the unique domain of a particular class of professionals. It has become the concern and responsibility of everyone. Security has become elusive. Military power, formerly a servant of definable goals, is increasingly treated as a goal in itself. Other values are subordinated to power in search of security.

Competition in war technology is an institutionalized routine of peace-time government fed by political, technological, economic and bureaucratic factors. The pursuit of power and security has become the overriding priority of government. Nuclear weapons may be considered either the crown of human technological creation or a final revelation of our ultimate depravity. In either case, they have profoundly changed the nature of war.

Modern war imposes a burden on society that is unprecedented in history. The new elements in modern war require a change in the way we think about war. Christian ethics cannot evade this change but must rethink the meaning of war in our modern world.

1 Roland H.Bainton, *Christian Attitudes to War and Peace* (Nashville: Abingdon, 1960), p. 185.

2 Walter Dorn, "European Militarism" in Gordon B. Turner, ed., *A History of Military Affairs* (New York: Harcourt Brace, 1952), p. 3.

3 Hoffman Nickerson, "Mass War Begins," ibid., p. 43.

4 Anatol Rapoport, *Conflict in a Man-Made Environment* (Baltimore: Penguin 1974), p. 218.

5 Ibid., p. 218.

6 Nickerson, p. 50.

7 Quoted in Nickerson, p. 39.

8 Rapoport, p. 219. See Carl Von Clausewitz, *On War*, Michael Howard and Peter Paret, eds. & trans. (Princeton, N.J.: Princeton University Press, 1976), Ch. 11

9 Edward Meade Earle, "The Influence of Air Power on History," in Turner, p. 601.

10 Ibid., pp. 605-606.

11 Ibid. p. 606.

12 Harold D. Lasswell, "The Garrison State Hypothesis Today," in Samuel P. Huntington, ed., *Changing Patterns of Military Politics* (New York: The Free Press of Glencoe, 1962), p. 55.

13 Rapoport, p. 220.

14 Ibid., p. 220.

15 Robert J. Lifton studied this phenomenon in detail from a psychological perspective. The term he uses to describe it is "psychic numbing." See *The Broken Connection* (New York: Simon and Schuster, 1979).

16 See Jacques Ellul, *The Technological Society* (New York: Vintage Books, 1964), pp. 78-147. Ellul's gloomy view of the omnipotence of "technique" in modern culture is profound in its broad outlines but simplistic because of his tendency to over-generalize.

17 Quincy Wright, *The Study of International Relations* (New York: Appleton-Century-Crofts, 1955), p. 373.

18 This point has been made by many authors including Wright, ibid., Ellul, p. 89, and Jonathan Schell, *The Fate of the World* (New York: Alfred A. Knopf, 1982).

19 Rapoport, p. 73.

20 World Council of Churches study document "Christians and the Prevention of War in an Atomic Age." 1958, #65.

21 Lasswell, p. 53.

22 Ibid, p. 60.

23 Rapoport, p. 221.

24 Albert Wohlstetter, "Is There a Strategic Arms Race?" Foreign Policy, No. 15 (Summer, 1974), pp. 3-20 and No. 16 (Fall, 1974), pp. 48-81. See also articles by Holst and Nacht, No. 19 (Summer, 1975), pp. 170-198.

25 Les Aspin, "What Are the Russians Up To?" *International Security,* No. 1 (Summer 1978) : 30-54.

26 From a speech by McNamara on September 18, 1967 in which he announced plans to deploy a limited ballistic missile defense system (A.B.M.) called "Sentinel." This system geared against a Chinese ballistic missile attack.

27 Ted Greenwood, *Making the MIRV: A Study of Defense Decision Making* (Cambridge, Mass.: Ballinger, 1975), p. 81. See also Colin S. Gray, "Action and Reaction in the Nuclear Arms Race," *Military Review,* 51 (Aug. 1971): 16-26.

28 John Steinbrunner, "Beyond Rational Deterrence: The Struggle for New Conceptions," *World Politics,* 28, No. 2 (Jan. 1976): 228.

29 Greenwood, p. 151.

CHAPTER II

FOUR MORAL APPROACHES TO WAR IN
THE HISTORY OF JUST WAR THEORY

The history of Christian ethical thought about war has been dominated by just war theory. To grapple with the unique problems of modern war, we must consider the moral approaches to war in the past. In this chapter we will examine four major periods of just war theory that continue to influence thinking about war today.

The first of these periods is represented by the Roman writer Cicero. Cicero's thought was deeply influenced by natural law thinking and the universalism of stoic philosophy.

Augustine's theologically conceived just war theory is the second major approach. Augustine's writings are an eloquent denunciation of war as well as a provisional justification of its political necessity.

The third kind of thinking about war drew heavily from Augustine's thought, but reduced it to an elaborate code of rules. Legalistic just war theory roughly coincided with the rise and fall of Christendom in Europe.

The breakdown of Christendom and the rise of the nation-state led to a fourth kind of just war theory that deemphasized the justifiability of war and concentrated on rational means of restraining its destructiveness. The result was an emphasis on rules of war based on the reciprocal self-interest of the parties involved.

Strictly speaking, just war theory is not a "theory" at all, but a set of normative and empirical assumptions from which proceeds both a qualified justification of warfare and a set of moral principles for its limitation. The term "theory" is so commonly used in the literature that I will continue to use it in the traditional, imprecise sense of "a system of thought."

Cicero: Just War Theory as a Strategy for Moral Empire

The first great proponent of a universal theory of justifiable war was the Roman political philosopher Cicero (106 B.C.-43 B.C.). The influence of Cicero on Western political and moral theory is profound. At the center of Cicero's thought was the Stoic conception of natural law. According to him, all people are subject to the eternal principles of natural law and justice. While Plato and Aristotle proposed rules for the moral restraint of suffering in warfare, both saw them as applying only to socially equal Greeks. Only war between "brothers" warranted moral restraint. From the foundation of universal natural law, Cicero developed the first comprehensive theory of just war intended to apply to all wars and all situations. Cicero's theory included rules to judge the justifiability of resorting to war *(jus ad bellum)*, and rules to judge the morality of specific practices of warfare *(jus in bello)*.

Cicero understood war as a result of the breakdown of reason. He says, "Although reason is characteristic of men and force of beasts, you must resort to force if there is no opportunity to employ reason. Therefore, wars should be undertaken only so that one may live in peace without wrongdoing."[1]

There is an unresolved tension in Cicero's thought between the cosmopolitan universalism implied in his natural law theory and his patriotic conviction that Roman law and ideals were the embodiment of natural law. In theory, Cicero's priorities are unambiguous. "... our first duty is to the immortal gods, our second, to country; our third, to parents; and so on, in a descending scale, to the rest."[2] Cicero clearly states that evil should never be done, even to save one's country. The gods, or natural law are above the state.

One the other hand, Cicero believed the Roman state was the highest human embodiment of natural law. Thus any war which upheld the state's honor and reputation was a just war. "We ought", said Cicero, "to be more prepared to wage war over honor and reputation than over advantages of other sorts."[3] Cicero's belief that all people are equal before natural law was in conflict with his conviction that Rome was destined to rule the world. Thus Cicero posits two different kinds of wars: wars for survival and wars for the glory of supremacy.

Wars in which the object is the glory of supremacy should be waged less bitterly. To draw an analogy, we fight with a fellow citizen in one way if he is a declared enemy, in another if he is merely a rival. With the latter the struggle concerns honor and office, with the former it involves life and reputation.[4]

It is hard to reconcile wars for the glory of supremacy with Cicero's emphasis on impartial, universal standards of justice in which war is only undertaken to preserve the peace without wrongdoing. Presumably natural reason should have led all nations to submit to the Roman yoke without force.

Cicero's equation of the natural order with the Roman empire makes it remarkable that he built a just war theory of immense influence on Western political thought. For Cicero, just war theory was a necessary part of natural law theory. International relations were as much a part of the natural order as personal relations.

For no phase of life, whether public or private, whether in business or in the home... can be without its moral duty; on the discharge of such duties depends all that is morally right and on their neglect all that is morally wrong.[5]

Bonkovsky says of Cicero's thought,

On the basis of the unity of mankind, international society could be asserted. To preserve it, justice had to be done. This justice, the standard of interpersonal and domestic relations, had also to be the rule of inter-state dealings.[6]

Cicero's primary point is that a just war must have as its goal the establishment of a just peace. The problem lies in the definition of just peace. War was considered just only if waged under the confines of Roman law. Cicero pointed out that, "Roman fetial law...makes it clear that no war is just unless it is waged after the government has demanded restitution or unless the war is previously announced and declared."

Revolutions were by definition unjust as they did not have state approval. Cicero acknowledged that there are unjust, state declared wars, but these are unlawful because they are "begun from a mad impulse without legitimate cause."[7]

Cicero's major concern was that war should be waged in an honorable fashion towards other states. Like Plato he distinguished between the guilty and the innocent among the enemy, but he did not specify that non-combatants were to be spared. In victory, he said, "You should spare those enemies who were not cruel or barbarous in warfare."[8] Cicero felt that a liberal peace was the only solid basis for the building of an empire. In war as in peace one should be guided by the principle of "humanitas." Humanitas includes such things as decorum, civility, refinement, benevolence, magnanimity and mercy.[9]

The state, even another foreign state, must not be dishonored by infidelity to an oath. Cicero observed, "There is also the law of war. Your fidelity to an oath often has to be maintained with an enemy."[10] But this is only true of a state enemy.

> For example, if you do not give to some pirates the ransom you agreed upon for your life, there is no deceit. Not even if you agreed under oath to pay a ransom. By definition a pirate is not on the list of fair enemies but rather is everyone's common enemy.[11]

Wars may only be legally fought by those who are appointed by the state. Cicero quoted Marcus Cato the elder as saying, "It is not lawful for someone who is not a soldier to fight a state enemy."[12] The individual may not do what is the state's duty to do, even if the cause is just.

Cicero was not uncritical of Rome's conduct in war. In the early days, according to Cicero, "One could more truly call Roman domination the protector of the world, not a ruler." He then proceeded to list some of her latter crimes such as the sack of Corinth, and concluded, "... I could mention many other crimes against our allies... We are being punished justly."[13]

Cicero was aware of the excessive cruelty that sometimes occurs in war. He observed that expediency sometimes leads to breaking of natural law. "In the government the securing of an apparent advantage very frequently causes wrongdoing as the Romans did wrong in the sack of Corinth." He went on to say, "Nothing is advantageous that is barbarous; barbarity is extremely repugnant to the nature of human being, and we ought to follow nature."[14]

Cicero viewed Roman warfare as a glorious activity. Yet his commitment to a universal, rational ethic is the prominent feature of his writing. When viewed against the backdrop of the classical world, Cicero had a remarkably humane view of warfare. His respect for the "natural equality" of all people, Roman or non-Roman, was a great improvement over the parochialism of Plato and Aristotle. The greatness of Cicero's thought is related to the universalism of his vision.

If Cicero's just war theory is applied to modern war, his universalism creates severe problems. Today one of the most serious causes of international conflict is the clash of opposing universal ideologies. The defense and propagation of a particular ideology, (whether Islam, or Marxism, or Capitalism), is a source of great danger in a world armed with nuclear weapons. Universalistic belief systems are not in themselves a cause of war. But when ideology is linked to military confrontation between nuclear powers, the whole world holds its breath. Cicero's emphasis on the glory of the state as the highest possible value is reminiscent of the ideological absolutism of some political leaders today. Such "statism" is a recipe for disaster.

While Cicero had immense influence, it is Augustine who articulated a just war theory that has dominated Christian thinking for 1500 years.

Augustine: Just War Theory in Tension

Augustine (354-430 A.D.) is often thought of as the first careful architect of a just war theory. Seen against the background of the pacifism of the pre-Constantinian church, he may indeed be considered a justifier of war. Augustine lived on the brink of destruction of the Roman Empire. Rome had been sacked and the Vandals were about to invade Africa. The Roman legions were the only hindrance to the destruction of civilization as Augustine knew it. This crisis fathered in Augustine the justification of defensive war.

If compared to the majority view of the post-Constantinian Church, Augustine appears strongly anti-war. Both Jerome and Ambrose saw Rome and Christianity as joint works of God.[15] Roman conquest produced the *Pax Romana* which was thought to realize all the hopes for peace of the Old and New Testaments. Bainton records that, "The practice of early Christianity was so far reversed by the early fifth century that under Theodosius II, those polluted by pagan rites were excluded from the army—only Christians could serve."[16] The view that Rome was God's instrument to usher in the kingdom of God could not stand up under the Barbarian invasion. Augustine not only saw that Rome could not bear the weight of being God's agent of temporal salvation, he also unmasked the horror of war and domination that had produced and sustained the empire.

Augustine can be seen in an even more radical light when compared with classical thinkers. Like Plato and Cicero, Augustine saw war as a fact of life. Unlike them, he never saw it as an honorable, let alone glorious activity. Nor was Augustine's just war theory simply a Christianization of Cicero's natural law thinking. Augustine's thought was born in the crucible of strongly conflicting elements in his mind. Augustine struggled to synthesize the rigorous demands of Christian love with a keen understanding of political realities and a pessimistic view of human nature.

The Origins and Causes of War

The primal roots of war, according to Augustine, lie in the original rebellion and fall of humanity. The Fall brought sin into the world which is the cause of all war. As a result of the Fall,

These mortals run to such enormities in sin that even the

beasts devoid of rational will...would live more securely and peaceably with their own kind than men... For not even lions or dragons have ever waged with their kind such wars as men have waged with one another.[17]

The founder of the earthly city, according to Augustine, was a fratricide. Cain, who represents the earthly city, killed Abel, who represents the heavenly city.[18] Thus it is no surprise that Romulus killed his brother Remus at the founding of Rome.

Augustine traced the growth of the Roman Empire through its wars of conquest. These wars, he believed, were initially "just" in that they were provoked by unjust neighbors. The Romans were first propelled by love of liberty. This love was soon overtaken by love of domination due to their desire for praise and thirst for glory. Augustine commented,

At that time it was their greatest ambition either to die bravely or to live free; but when liberty was obtained, so great a desire of glory took possession of them that liberty alone was not enough unless domination also should be sought.[19]

"God did not intend," Augustine lamented, "that his rational creature, who was made in His image, should have dominion over anything but the irrational creation—not man over man but man over beasts."[20] To Augustine, war enslaved not only the loser but the winner. He said, "It is a happier thing to be the slave of a man than of a lust; for even this very lust of ruling...lays waste men's hearts with the most ruthless dominion."[21]

The love of glory and domination is fundamentally a rejection of God and his role. Augustine saw the lack of worship of God as the root of all evil. Love of God and neighbor cannot be separated, so this rejection of God is played out through domination of others. "It is thus that pride in its perversity apes God. It abhors equality with other men under him; but instead of his rule it seeks to impose a rule of its own upon equals."[22]

Finally, Augustine echoes the classical affirmation that wars are fought for the sake of peace. Peace, in some sense, is the motive behind even the most criminal and violent acts.

> Even wicked men wage war to maintain the peace of their own circle, and wish that if possible all men belonged to them, that all men and things might serve but one head, and might either through love or fear yield themselves to peace with him.[23]

This kind of peace is a perversion of what God intended. Nevertheless, one cannot blot out the God-given instinct for peace. Pride

> abhors... the just peace of God and loves its own unjust peace; but it can't help loving peace of one kind or other. For there is no vice so clean contrary to nature that it obliterates even the faintest traces of nature.[24]

For Augustine, the motive of peace did not in itself justify warfare, No evil has an existence of its own but rather is a perversion and parasite of good. War feeds on and is nourished by the hope for peace.

War and the Nature of the State

Augustine held two paradoxical views of the state. On the one hand, the state is ordained by God and as such is the instrument of his justice. Indeed the Roman Empire came about at the will of God and not by chance or fate. As God's instrument of justice, Augustine conceded to the state a right to wield the sword which could never be right for the individual Christian.

> They who have waged war in obedience to the divine command or in conformity with His laws have represented in their persons the public justice or the wisdom of government, and in this capacity have put to death wicked men; such men have by no means violated the commandment, 'Thou shalt not kill.'[25]

Augustine would not allow even the barest self-defense for the Christian as an individual. Delegated by the state, justice could be accomplished by killing. Yet even here the magistrate must love and sorrow in his heart while exercising the authority of the state to punish. Hence, Augustine's famous "mournful magistrate."

In tension with this view of the state, Augustine denied that any earthly state was founded on justice. The fundamental criterion of justice, according to Augustine, is worship of the only true God. Augustine rejected Cicero's requirement that a state must be just in order to be a true state.

He defined a state as a group of people who have a common agreement, and thus conceded that Rome was a state. But he suggested, "Justice being taken away, then, what are kingdoms but great robberies?"[26] The Roman Empire had survived, according to Augustine, "... even though unjust, for justice is not necessary for its being, as Cicero held, but only for its well being. A robber band has the essential features of a state."[27] Augustine illustrated his point with the story of Alexander the Great asking a robber what he meant by keeping hostile possession of the sea. The pirate replied, "What thou meanest by seizing the whole earth? But because I do it with a petty ship, I am called a robber, whilst thou who dost it with a great fleet art styled emperor."[28]

Augustine relativized all power and rule. Final allegiance must be to God alone. Exceptional wars may be justly waged by the state but wars are not just because the state wages them. With Augustine's requirement of love in the heart of every soldier, it is hard to see how a just war could have occurred, even in his day.

Augustine mourned the cost that had been levied for the *Pax Romana.* "But the imperial city has endeavored to impose on subject nations not only her yoke, but her language, as a bond of peace....but how many great wars, how much slaughter and bloodshed have provided this unity."[29] Augustine had maintained that, "An attack on the existence of a state was ordinarily an injury to be repulsed by war, but not always. Honor is preferred to safety. But usually divine law permits self-defense to states."[30] This qualified right of defense is a far cry from the use of force to increase the glory and honor of the state.

The Just War

Augustine's consideration of how a war may be justified grew out of the desperate situation of the invasion of the Vandals. Augustine assumed that a just war would be waged defensively. Defense is not primarily of the person fighting but of all the inhabitants of the land. Augustine also presupposed that the aggressor would be wrong and the just war party right. "For it is the wrong doing of the opposing party which compels the wise man to wage just wars."[31] Augustine believed that attitude rather than action is fundamental to the Christian ethic of love. If the heart remains pure, what is done of necessity by the body may be justified.

Augustine's major concern was a Christian justification for fighting in a war. Thus his major focus is on *jus ad bellum*. Augustine saw the just conduct of a war *(jus in bello)*, as one of the criteria by which a war may be justified or condemned. There are five principles which Augustine believed were applicable to both the justification and the just conduct of war. These points were not presented as a list of rules or as a cohesive theory but are scattered throughout his writings.[32]

Augustine's first point directly concerned the attitude of an officer who questioned whether a Christian could fight. Writing to General Boniface, Augustine urged him to withstand the Vandal invasion of Africa, but stated,

> Peace should be the object of your desire. War should be waged only as a necessity... Therefore even in the course of war you should cherish the spirit of a peace maker.[33]

This first point echoed the classic belief that war should be waged for peace, but added the Augustinian inward motivation. The second point was that wars must have a just cause. "Those wars may be defined as just, " said Augustine, "which avenge injuries."[34] What sort of injuries? Primarily Augustine meant an attack on the existence of the state, although even this did not guarantee that a war was just.

The inward attitude of love was a third requirement for a war to be just. Love, argued Augustine, is not incompatible with killing because it is an attitude of the heart, not an action.

> If it is supposed that God could not enjoin warfare be-
> cause... Jesus said... "Resist not evil"... the answer, is that
> what is here required is not a bodily action but an inward
> disposition.... Moses, in putting to death sinners, was not
> moved by cruelty but by love. Love does not preclude a be-
> nevolent severity nor that correction which compassion it-
> self dictates.[35]

Augustine made this ethic of love almost beyond the pale
of human wartime virtue by stating, "No one indeed is fit to
inflict punishment save the one who has first overcome hate in
his heart. The love of enemy admits of no dispensation, but
love does not exclude wars of mercy waged by the good."[36]

Augustine considered the use of force coupled with an
attitude of love possible for those in public authority but not
for the private Christian citizen. The individual citizen must
not defend him or herself, even from robbery, rape or murder,
not because it would not be just but because a person cannot do so
without passion, self-assertion and a loss of love.

> As to killing others to defend one's own life, I do not
> approve of this, unless one happens to be a soldier or a
> public functionary acting not for himself but in defense of
> others or of the city in which he resides.[37]

Augustine's fourth point was that a war should be just in its
auspices, i.e. waged under the authority of a legitimate ruler
or government.

Finally, Augustine echoed Plato and Cicero in insisting
that the conduct of war must be just. Faith must be kept with
the enemy; there should be no wanton violence, no profaning of
temples, looting massacre, or burning. Though Augustine
permitted ambush, he denounced vengeance, "all atrocities"
and reprisals.

Realism and the Horror of War

Augustine was the first Western writer to deny that there
is honor in any war. The horror of all war was a frequent

theme in his writing. "But say they, the wise man will wage just wars. As if he would not all the rather lament the necessity of just wars, if he remembers that he is a man."[38] War was the greatest of all evils to Augustine.

> Let everyone who thinks with pain on these great evils, so horrible, so ruthless, acknowledge that this is misery. And if anyone either endures or thinks of them without mental pain, this is a more miserable plight still, for he thinks himself happy because he has lost human feeling.[39]

The words "glory" and "victory" are evil masks that hide the true character of warfare. Asked Augustine, "Why allege to me the mere names and words of "glory" and "victory"? Tear off the disguise of wild delusion, and look at the naked deeds; weigh them naked, judge them naked."[40] The Roman Empire was an ugly crime against humanity. "This lust of sovereignty disturbs and consumes the human race with frightful ills. By this lust Rome was overcome when she triumphed over Alba and, praising her own crime, called it glory."[41] The idea that a person was great because he fought and conquered was ludicrous to Augustine.

Augustine doubted that any war can bring lasting peace. Even the noblest and best intentioned victory cannot keep peace for long. "Of this calamitous history we have no small proof, in the fact that no subsequent king has closed the gates of war."[42]

The man of war, said Augustine, is worse than a slave because he is ruled by lust.

> What prudence is there in wishing to glory in the greatness and extent of the empire, when you cannot point out the happiness of men, who are always rolling with dark fear and cruel lust in warlike slaughters and in blood, which, whether shed in civil or foreign war is still human blood.[43]

When Africa was on the verge of invasion by the Vandals, only the Roman legions stood in the way. At the head of the Romans was a Christian general whose wife had just died and who wished to retire and become a monk. "Not now," pleaded

Augustine.

> The monks indeed occupy a higher place before God. But
> you should not aspire to their blessedness before the
> proper, time...the monks will pray for you against your
> invisible, enemies. You must fight for them against the
> Barbarians, their visible foes.[44]

The religious, the secular clergy and the monks must not,
according to Augustine, engage in any warfare at all but must
practice completely the counsels of perfection. But not all
Christians were bound to be perfect. Augustine saw war as an
evil necessity of the city of man which Christians may be
required to partake in, that the earthly city might endure and
provide a cradle in which the heavenly city might grow.

The universal outrage that Augustine expressed towards
war is a welcome addition to ancient moral literature which
was certainly more familiar with the terms of honor and
fatalism than compassion and love. Augustine's hatred of war
is almost matched by his longing for peace. His concept of
peace, however, owes more to the Hebrews than to the Greeks.
Peace was not simply the absence of conflict, but the "perfectly
ordered, harmonious enjoyment of God and one another in
God."[45] This peace is the true end of humanity and will come
when the human city is swallowed up by the city of God.
Augustine believed that, in a fallen world where God is
rejected, war is a tragic fact which must be recognized. The
Christian must judge on the basis of love between greater and
lesser evils. War remains an evil necessity which may or may
not be justified by the presence of even greater evils.

Augustine's just war theory may by seen as a synthesis of
elements from his Christian background, his classical
education and his existential response to his own political
context. From Christian theology Augustine drew a somber
view of human sin and a pessimistic view of history. He
clearly distinguished between "this world" and the "Kingdom
of God."

This led to a distinction in his thought between political
responsibility and perfect love. Augustine did not consider
these two as polarities. Love is to rule responsibly and be

incarnated in just political action. This was only possible through a radical emphasis on love as an inward disposition. Augustine's political ethics heavily rely on subjective intent. Augustine knew that the tension between responsibility and the Gospel could never be fully resolved, so he emphasized the distinction between different callings.

Varying demands are placed upon the ruler, the soldier, the citizen, and the cleric or monk. Only the cleric or monk is bound by the "counsel of perfection." Augustine acknowledged political necessity without making it normative. His ultimate allegiance was to God, whatever the consequences. Augustine's acknowledgement of necessity is strongly modified by his commitment to an ethic of love and personal non-resistance.

From Cicero and the classics, Augustine drew an emphasis on the common good, the idea of natural rights and of just war. Augustine both relativized and valued the state, but like Cicero he saw the fall of the state as a great calamity.

As a high-born Roman citizen, Augustine's respect for the state was also a legacy of his cultural context. If Augustine had been a Barbarian convert experiencing Roman exploitation he might have held different views. The complexity of Augustine's view was certainly influenced by the emergence of the Church from political persecution and the apparent Christianization of the empire. With the ascent of the Christian emperors, Constantine and Theodosius, it must have appeared possible for Rome to become a just state. The pagans taunted Christians that Rome was falling because of Christianity. The pressure to formulate a just war theory to legitimize defense of the Christian empire must have been immense.

The tension Augustine expressed between the radical requirements of a Christian ethic of love and a responsible approach to political necessities has not been relieved but intensified by changes in the nature of war. An adequate political ethic must not resolve one side of the tension at the expense of the other. Augustine attempted to account for both by personalizing an ethic of perfection and relating it to political responsibility through an emphasis on interior intention.

The political ethic I propose in chapter six is indebted to Augustine's definition of the problem. A separation between an ideal ethic and political responsibility is necessary in a fallen world. However, Augustine's solution to the problem he perceived does not do justice to the unique calling of all Christians in relation to a pluralistic society.

The Third Stage: Just War Theory as a Code of Rules

In the Middle Ages just war theory became systematized and codified. Very few significant new ideas were added to the theory that were not already stated by Cicero and Augustine, The process of codification produced a legalistic approach to Augustine's ideas that was far less profound than Augustine's nuanced thought. It is difficult to measure the impact of just war codes during the Middle Ages. For the most part they were ignored. Their effectiveness varied with political conditions.

The political context of Europe following Augustine was anarchic. Wars between various houses of the nobility abounded. The Barbarians, who took over the Roman Empire, embraced Christianity and in the process militarized it. Christ became a battle cry and the just war theory was ignored. Christianity was split into many warring groups by schisms and intrigues. Ideological fragmentation snuffed out the universal ideals upon which just war theory was founded.

Probably the threat of Islam, more than anything else, influenced unification in the empire. The spreading power of Islam prompted crusades in the 11th, 12th and 13th centuries. With the crusades came a growth in the idea of Christendom and its accompanying ideology and culture. Sometimes the very leaders who most vigorously promoted the Crusades were peacemakers when it came to war within Europe. St. Bernard of Clairvaux preached holy war against the infidels as a means of atoning for sins. His efforts also limited and restrained war between Christian princes.

War between "Christians" was often extremely brutal. As the idea of Christendom developed there were increasing efforts by the Church to limit and soften the effects of war. The "Peace of God" (990 AD) and the "Truce of God" (1085) were two attempts to limit the violence of "just wars."

The Peace of God decreed, on pain of excommunication, that there should be no violence against various classes of non-combatants. Church property, which was considerable, was also declared off-limits to warfare. The Truce of God extended the Peace of God by prohibiting warfare on holy days and specific weekdays. The total of these days left about a quarter of the year for fighting. The church was also active in the arbitration of disputes. Between 1200 and 1450 there were over a hundred recorded cases of formal arbitration.

Even though the results of these attempts at regulating just war were somewhat disappointing, they did have some effect. In 1148 Gratian's *Decretals* came out as an official attempt to define a "just war." Gratian draws heavily from Augustine and adds very little. His main emphasis is on the *jus ad bellum* question of how war can be valid for a Christian. Gratian defines just war both as a means to avenge wrongs and as a means to coerce the enemies of the Church. But he rules out preventive or punitive wars.

About a hundred years later, Raymond of Pennaforte organized Augustine's ideas into five rules for the determination of a just war: 1. just persons (no clergy), 2. just object (to redress real injury), 3. just cause (including last resort in the establishment of justice), 4. just intention (motivated by justice, not hate) and 5. valid authority. These rules are clear but rigid. Like Augustine, the schoolmen regarded war as a *prima facie* evil but they lacked the profundity of his historical perspective.

Thomas Aquinas (1225-1274) also added little to Augustine. Aquinas recommended that Augustine should be read. Aquinas emphasized right authority, just cause and right intention. Right authority was a particularly important point in the Middle Ages because of the anarchic chaos of feudalism and the assumption of divine right behind legitimate authority. Right authority sought to stop feudal lords from going to war over every grievance.

Aquinas offered one major innovation of just war theory by applying to personal defense Augustine's ethic of intention. He circumvented Augustine's emphasis on complete, personal non-resistance by legitimizing self-defense on the basis of the doctrine of "double effect". Thomas suggested that an individual Christian may kill an unjust attacker if the intention of the Christian is only to repel him. Directly intended lethal defense is not permissible to the individual Christian. But if one only intends to repel the assailant and the person is killed, the killing is only an unfortunate side effect and not morally wrong.

Aquinas did not extend the double effect doctrine into the conduct of war. He assumed that directly intended killing of an unjust enemy was permissible. And it was unlikely that, with the limited war technology of the thirteenth century, "innocent" bystanders would be killed as an unintended side effect. The only glimmering of a principle of non-combatant immunity in Aquinas is his argument that clergy should not fight or be attacked.

Augustine had a far more restrictive doctrine of double effect. Augustine argued that even soldiers in a just war should let necessity, and not their will, kill the enemy. Augustine uses an ethic of intention and double effect as a further restriction on the limited permission for Christian soldiers to fight. Aquinas uses it to give permission for limited self-defense. Neither anticipated its later extension to justify the use of increasingly destructive technology.

James Johnson observes that, "In 1340, at the start of the Hundred Years War, both sides could still reasonable believe in war as a corporate trial by battle in which God would grant victory to the side with justice behind its claims."[46] Warfare prior to the Hundred Years War was relatively mild. Truces were strictly kept and there was an unwritten code of chivalry which ameliorated the suffering of war.

Ecclesiastical just war writers had mainly concentrated on *jus ad bellum* with the assumption that war was wrong and at least questionable for Christians. However the chivalric code glorified war as a God-given means of righting wrong. Writers like Honore Bonet, drawing form the chivalric tradition, assumed the *jus ad bellum* categories and concentrated primarily on *jus in bello*. The protection of the innocent was a central concern of chivalry. Hence Bonet drew up a long and elaborate list of non-combatants. War was only to be fought by knights, who were required to be virtuous men.

The chaotic Middle Ages not only prompted the rise of just war theory, it also gave rise to various pacifist movements. Within the Catholic Church monastic orders which shunned worldly conflict flourished.

The Franciscans were able to remain in the Church as a semi-pacifist movement which followed the "counsels of perfection." Other less diplomatic pacifist movements such as the Waldenses, the Lollards, the Hussites and the Moravian Brethren were forced into a sectarian stance which foreshadowed the Reformation.

By the late 15th century there was a highly elaborate just war code with rules governing both *jus ad bellum* and *jus in bello*. In Italy during the early Renaissance of the late 15th and early 16th centuries, just war theory seemed very effective.[47] Prior to the invasion by Charles VIII of France, wars were very mild and gentlemanly. In important battles sometimes few or even no people were killed. War consisted of orderly, rule-governed skirmishes in which bargaining took place by the taking of prisoners. The Peace of God and the Truce of God were widely observed. War was fought on horseback with hand wielded weapons. Cannons were despised as dishonorable and sub-human.

This remarkable period was not, unfortunately, due to the triumph of just war ideals. Nor was it characteristic of all Europe. A unique set of circumstances combined to mitigate the brutality of war. The unifying acceptance of "Christendom" provided a common culture and ideology in which independent sovereign states recognized each others right to exist. Both the Church and the Empire were weak and there was a rough balance of power between the five Italian states. Only the high-born were involved in warfare and all parties had a vested interest in preserving the social fabric upon which their own wealth and power were based. Non- combatants and their value as productive units were the property over which war was fought. There existed no expedient reason to destroy them. With the military power of the states roughly balanced and resources of the city-states stretched already, large scale military conflict was too expensive to be worthwhile. This does not mean that life for the peasants was easy or just—only that war between knights was mild and just war theory was observed in practice.

Most of the recent discussion of just war theory revolves around the code of rules that was developed in the Middle Ages.

The Development toward Modern Just War Doctrine

Just war theory up to the Renaissance was formulated within the context of a unified ideology of Christendom. By the time the Spanish Scholastics addressed the problem of war, the political and ideological situation had shifted radically.[48] The emergence of diverse, secular, nation-states challenged both the authority of the Church and the viability of Christendom. The authority of any binding, universal moral norms was called into question. The diverse fragmentation of the Reformation also undermined the cultural unity of Europe. At the same time the conquest of the Americans raised new questions about warfare against non-Christian peoples.

Another factor which prompted a rethinking of just war theory was the brutality of the Wars of Religion during the 16th century. Alongside the clamor for the holy war came a growing realization that something was wrong when all parties claimed justice for their side and prayed to the Christian God for victory.

These changes prompted a shift in the internal structure and areas of emphasis in just war doctrine. Franciscus De Vittoria, and Francisco Suarez began this shift with their insistence that different religions were not a just cause for war. Vittoria argued that belief cannot be coerced. War to convert infidels, (i.e. Indians in the New World), was invalid because both sides in the fighting would be, from their perspective, fighting a just war. Vittoria suggested that defense against aggression was an inviable principle of natural law. Therefore the Indians would be right to defend themselves. If both sides had justice on their side then neither could legitimately kill the other. But Vittoria also treated the right to trade as part of natural law. If the Indians attacked the traders, the traders could legitimately respond in kind.

Vittoria and Suárez upheld the traditional concept that, in the eyes of God, only one side could be right in a just war. Therefore, according to Vittoria a prince must be absolutely sure of a just cause before going to war. On the other hand Vittoria recognized the problem of "invincible ignorance." One's opponent may not be capable of knowing your cause in just. If this is the case, just war must be waged very carefully with scrupulous attention to *jus in bello*. Suarez further insisted that the *jus in bello* rules for the conduct of war were universal and binding on Christian and non- Christian princes alike.

The major shift in just war thinking was only partially the rejection of ideologically justified wars. More important was a growing emphasis on *jus in bello* categories at the expense of *jus ad bellum*.

As nation-states claimed both autonomy and sovereignty over their own actions it became apparent that there was no objective authority which could pronounce one side just and the other unjust. Both sides in a conflict usually claimed to have reasonable justification for going to war. This did not mean that *jus ad bellum* did not exist. In the eyes of God one side might be primarily right and the other primarily wrong. But the moralists recognized that practical emphasis on just conduct within war was more fruitful for the limitation of war than the subjective discussions of justice.

Spanish scholastics emphasized the now classic principles of proportionality and discrimination as governing the conduct of war. Proportionality was defined as a just relation between the ends and the means of warfare. Discrimination was the principle that only the guilty could be attacked. The innocent, those without any direct contribution to the war effort, were to be spared.

Vittoria and Suarez extended Aquinas' double effect doctrine and allowed killing the innocent when it is an unavoidable side effect. An example given was the use of a cannon in the siege of a city. The control of indiscriminate weapons is left to subjective judgement. Likewise the principle of proportionality is never closely defined. Vittoria and Suarez left the specifics of *jus in bello* to be determined by the *jus gentium. Jus gentium* was defined as the customary practice among nations.[49] Proportionality and discrimination were considered universal principles of natural law. The practical definition of what they meant in relation to specific tactics must be determined contextually with attention to tradition and reciprocity between nations.

A major step in the direction of the secularization of just war doctrine was made by Hugo Grotius. A Dutch thinker who wrote a few years later than Suarez. Grotius attempted to distinguish between what can reasonably be deduced from nature and what is permitted to Christians.

In the first part of his tract on the *Law of Peace and War* Grotius sounded like a realist. He said, in effect, if a war is just, anything goes and is just. In his second section, Grotius set up strict absolute limits of moderation which he insisted are fundamental principles of natural law. The basis for just war doctrine must be a self-validating morality that is true, "even if there were no God, which God forbid."[50]

Because of his desire to build a secular doctrine that was not tied to religion, Grotius deemphasized the internal, subjective elements of just war theory. Grotius saw war as a human enterprise that was capable of being restrained. Government was not the minister of God but of the people. Grotius reduced the *jus ad bellum* categories to external, formal requirements for a just war. He rejected the requirement of just intention as too subjective. National sovereignty replaced right authority and the necessity of formal declaration was emphasized. In most wars, Grotius recognized that both sides could appear to meet these criteria. Thus the *jus in bello* categories became the principle marks of a just war.

The process of the secularization of just war theory reached its logical conclusion in the works of John Locke and Emmerich De Vattel, both of whom erected non-transgressable bounds for *jus in bello* without reference to a higher morality such as charity. Locke emphasized natural human rights not to be set aside, even in warfare. Vattel stressed the absolute responsibility of the sovereign for war and the relative innocence of non-combatants. Central to Vattel's analysis was the role of enlightened self-interest and reciprocity in the keeping of *jus in bello* principles.

Vattel is often called the father of international law. He suggested that the most effective way to set boundaries for international conduct is not through the assertion of moral principles but through reciprocal agreements which appeal to the self-interest of all involved. There is a problem with international law modeled on Vattel's suggestions. If the basis for agreement is reciprocal self-interest, and self-interest is threatened that agreement may be ignored.

Secularized just war theory which relies on conventions of reciprocal self-interest is extremely important in a pluralistic world in which there is no moral consensus. Adherence to the war convention is seldom based purely on self-interest. Moral habits and convictions influence decision makers. Not only self-interest but also world opinion has an impact. Unfortunately the secular just war doctrine that is embodied in international law is inadequate in relation to the dangers posed by modern war. Nor does international law address the fundamental moral questions with which Christians should be concerned. However, reciprocal self-interest is better than no rational restraint. One can only hope that the effectiveness of international law will be enhanced as nations perceive the dangers of modern war.

Conclusion

This has been a selective review of the landmark figures of just war doctrine. The major themes of the authors examined provide the foundation for just war thinking today.

The four stages of just war theory examined are a progression only in a historical sense.[51] In the first stage, exemplified by Cicero, the emphasis was on the promotion of a universal value system called natural law. The value of universal reason and justice were to be spread and maintained through just war.

This kind of just war theory is common today among those who would maintain or extend "freedom" or "democracy" or "socialism" or "The Revolution" through "just" military action against their opponents. The modern version of just war as a strategy for empire focuses on *jus ad bellum* and, unlike Cicero and Plato, neglects *jus in bello*. In this view the justice of the cause and the necessity of victory overrides scruples about specific tactics.

The most profound just war theory is found in the writings of Augustine. Augustine's theory starts with a recognition of both the dangers of an unbridled state and its necessity for maintaining order. Augustine's pessimism about human nature and history did not lead him to a fatalistic or cynical view of politics. Instead, he proposed that Christians realistically evaluate political necessity without abandoning their basic orientation in an ethic of love. His just war theory is thus primarily a *mode of reasoning* rather than a set of rules. Many currents in present day Roman Catholic just war theory exemplify this approach.

The third ideal type of just war theory, developed in the Middle Ages, elaborated Augustine's thought into a code or rules to provide a checklist both to determine what a just war was and to provide concrete principles for the limitation and control of war.

This type of reasoning was widely used during the Vietnam war to condemn U.S. involvement. As we will see in the next two chapters, there are substantial difficulties in applying the traditional rules to wars with modern technology.

In its fourth stage, the secularization of just war sought reasonable principles independent from any ideology. These principles would be reinforced by *reciprocal self-interest*.

In the modern period this approach has been demonstrated most clearly in the attempt to formulate international law. It is also prominent in the work of those who attempt to structure international agreements that will respect, for example, human rights. Just war theory based on reciprocal self-interest is a point where just war theory and political realism overlap.

Just war doctrine was undermined from four different directions. In the 16th century the just war mode of reasoning was extended into holy war concepts. With the disintegration of Christendom came renewed attempts to restore a common ideology and religion by force. Augustine's persecution of the Donatists was used as a justification for a crusading mentality.[52] War for religion then was akin to war for "democracy" today.

Secondly, just war theory was undermined by the tenacity of sectarian pacifist groups which survived in spite of persecution and challenged the legitimacy of the Christian use of violence.

Thirdly, the growing secularization of politics undermined the idea of a single set of moral rules that could regulate international behavior. The birth in Europe of secular realism was most clearly seen in the 16th century writings of Niccolo Machiavelli. As God and the Church came to be seen as less significant actors in successful politics, the idea of war as a rule governed activity became dispensable.

The changing nature of war itself most decisively undercut just war theory. As the technology of war became more and more destructive, it became increasingly difficult to sustain the logic of just war theory in the face of military "necessity."

Chapter three examines the revolution in moral and strategic thinking required by nuclear weapons.

1   Marcus Tullius Cicero, *De Officiis/On Duties*, Harry G. Edinger, trans. (New York: Bobbs-Merrill Co., 1974), I, (34), p. 19.

2   Ibid., I (160), p. 73.

3   Ibid., I (83), p. 39.

4   Ibid., (37), p. 20.

5   Ibid., I (4), p. 5.

6   Frederick O. Bonkovsky, *International Norms and National Policy* (Grand Rapids, Mich: Wm. B. Eerdmans, 1980), p. 17. Bonkovsky emphasizes that the origin of just war thinking is in Cicero, not Augustine. He exaggerates the consistence and thoroughness of Cicero's thought. He ignores the tension between Cicero's universal ideals and his intense patriotism. He also reads into Cicero some of the clear categories of later just war theory. The basic ideas may be implicit in Cicero's assumptions but they are not clear categories. Bonkovsky is very helpful in tracing the impact of political change on political theory.

7   Marcus Tullius Cicero, *On the Commonwealth*, G.H. Sabine and B.S. Smith, trans. (Indianapolis: Bobbs-Merrill Co., 1976), III (23), p. 217.

8   *De Officiis*, Book I (34), p.19.

9   See Roland H. Bainton, *Christian Attitudes to War and Peace* (Nashville: Abingdon Press), 1960, p. 41.

10   *De Officiis*, III, (107), p. 171.

11   Ibid. p. 171.

12   Ibid., I (37), p. 20.

13   Ibid., II (27), pp. 87-88.

14   Ibid., III, p. 141.

15   See Bainton, p. 87.

16   Ibid., p. 88.

17   Augustine, *The City of God*, Marcus Dods, trans., Great Books of the Western World, vol. 18 (Chicago: Encyclopaedia Britannica, 1957), Bk. XII, Ch. 22, p. 357.

18   Ibid., XV, Ch. 5. 400.

19   Ibid., V, Ch. 12.

20   Ibid., XIX, Ch. 15, p. 521.

21   Ibid.

22   Ibid., Ch. 12, p. 518.

23   Ibid.

24   Ibid.

25   Ibid., I, Ch. 21, p. 142.

26   Ibid., IV, Ch. 4, p. 190.

27   Ibid., XIX, Ch. 24, p. 528.

28   Ibid., Ch. 4, p. 190.

29 Ibid., XIX, Ch. 7, p. 515.
30 Augustine, *De Libero Arbitris*, V, Ch. 12.
31 *The City of God*, XIX, Ch. 7, p. 515.
32 The following passages were originally collected by Gustave Combes, *La Doctrine Politique de Saint Augustin*, Paris, 1927, and are quoted by Roland H. Bainton, pp. 95ff.
33 *Epist.* (189), p. 6.
34 *Quast. Help.*, IV, (10), C.E.S.I., XXVIII, (2), p. 428.
35 *Contra Faustum*, XXII, pp. 76 & 79. *Epist.*, 138, ii, 14.
36 *Sermo Dom*, I, XX, 63 & 70.
37 *Epist.*, 475.
38 *City of God*, XIS, Ch. 7, p. 515.
39 Ibid.
40 Ibid., III, Ch. 13, p. 174.
41 Ibid., p. 176.
42 Ibid., XIX, Ch. 14, p. 176.
43 Ibid., IV, Ch. 3, p. 190.
44 *Epist. 99*, CSEL, XXIV, pp. 533-34.
45 *City of God*, XIX, Ch. 11, p. 519.
46 James Turner Johnson, *Ideology, Reason, and the Limitation of War* (Princeton: Princeton University Press, 1975), p. 62.
47 See Bainton, Ch. 8.
48 See Leroy B. Walters, Jr., "Five Classic Just-War Theories: A Study in the Thought of Thomas Aquinas, Vittoria Suarez, Gentile and Grotius," (Ph.D. dissertation, Yale University, 1971), pp. 201-409.
49 See Johnson, p. 201.
50 See *De Ivre Belli ac Pacis*, Amsterdam, 1642, Prologue xx.
51 J. Bryan Hehir, also identifies four stages of development in just war theory. Hehir's stages of development are slightly different from mine because he starts with Augustine rather than Cicero. His fourth stage is modern papal teaching which I have not included. See, "The Just War Ethic and Catholic Theology" in Thomas A. Shannon, ed., *War or Peace? The Search for New Answers* (Maryknoll, N.Y.: Orbis, 1980).
52 Augustine's repression of the Donatists is better understood as political action that included elements of religious persecution than as a holy war.

CHAPTER III

THE IMPACT OF NUCLEAR WEAPONS
ON THE NATURE OF WAR

In chapter one we saw that the problem of war in the modern world is complex and goes far beyond the simple existence of nuclear weapons. Yet it is nuclear weapons that have revolutionized warfare more than all other products of technology combined. In this chapter we examine the way in which nuclear weapons have changed war.

Fundamentally the change is from war as a contest of strength to war as a bargaining process based on the manipulation of risk. In the first section we examine this change and the way it has transformed the relations between opponents in conflict.

The most obvious reason for changes in war is the incredible power of nuclear weapons. In the second section we examine the destructive capabilities of nuclear weapons. In separating fact from popular myth we see how thermonuclear bombs change the physical character of war.

The third section of this chapter examines the evolution of military strategy stimulated by nuclear armaments. The United States has made the transition from holding a nuclear monopoly to facing a roughly equal nuclear opponent. This transition has promoted several different strategies, each of which raises its own practical, moral and rational problems.

Finally, the strategies of nuclear defense raise grave problems concerning the meaning of rationality. We discuss some of the paradox and uncertainty that accompanies the attempt to formulate a rational strategy, particularly the relation between rationality and morality.

The Change in the Nature of War

War with nuclear weapons is a new phenomenon that must be rethought with new categories. The great nineteenth century thinker, Carl Von Clausewitz, defined six major elements of war as he knew it. The first three concerned application of force against the enemy. 1.) physical force: i.e. the number of soldiers that could be brought to bear on the enemy, 2.) morale: i.e. how well these soldiers can be induced to fight, and 3.) the strategic genius of the commanders in maneuvering their forces into superior fighting position.[1] The other three cited the natural barriers to the level of violence possible: 4.) the fragmented character of war—war never consists of a single blow, 5.) the "natural" superiority of defense over offense and 6.) "friction"—unforeseen and unpredictable difficulties in battle.[2]

All six of these classic elements remain and are applicable in their traditional sense to most conventional warfare. But none of them apply in the same sense to nuclear war. 1.) Physical force is no longer tied to manpower. With nuclear weapons the problem is not how to apply the maximum amount of force but how to *restrict* the amount of force and still gain an objective. 2.) Morale is no longer primarily related to the troops but is necessary for the whole society which must accept the suffering and guilt of the war. 3.) The genius of the commanders is less important in the maximum application of force than the careful restriction of violence. Potential violence is more useful than violence expended. 4.) The fragmented character of war is no longer a necessary barrier to violence. Virtually unlimited violence can now be unleashed in minutes. 5.) With nuclear weapons defense is no longer superior to offense. There is now an overwhelming advantage to striking first. Defense in the traditional sense is no longer even possible. 6.) The unforeseen and unpredictable difficulties of nuclear war are as likely to increase as much as impede the amount of violence done to the enemy. The unpredictable threatens not only the enemy but also the ecosystem of the earth.

In 1946 Bernard Brodie predicted:

Thus far the chief purpose of our military establishment has been to win wars. From now on its chief purpose must be to avert them. It can have almost no other useful purpose.[3]

In the past, commanders relied on their own experience and the recorded history of other wars to guide them in battle. There is no history of nuclear combat on which leaders can draw for guidance. Clausewitz saw war as a struggle against the natural limits of violence. Today there are virtually no limits and the struggle is with the control and restriction of violence. Thomas Hobbes suggested that nations faced each other like gladiators in a ring. Michael Mandelbaum suggests that the superpowers are most like fencers on a tight-rope. The image leaves out the fact that in Hobbes' day the gladiators were made up of the king and his military forces while today whole societies walk the tight-rope.

War used to be a contest of strength that took place when bargaining broke down. It would be an exaggeration to say that modern war is no longer a contest of strength. However, all modern war between superpowers is circumscribed by the fact that each has the ability to annihilate the other. Because of nuclear weapons, war between nuclear powers can never again be a simple contest of strength and endurance. It must be a bargaining process in which the final offensive weapon is the willingness to commit genocide and the final defense is the willingness to risk suffering it. War is no longer a contest of strength but a contest of suffering, will and restraint.

With the change from war as a contest of strength to war as a contest of violence, the greatest powers have become, in one sense, the most vulnerable. Military power used to signal a kind of security. In the nuclear age the great powers are the primary targets of a violence against which there is no physical defense. As Thomas Schelling observed, "Opposing strengths may cancel each other, pain and grief do not."[4]

Deterrence through threat of retaliation has always been an important part of military strategy. Deterrence today has become virtually the only defense against nuclear attack. Deterrence is now the central fact of modern military strategy.

This creates a shift from war as a primarily physical activity to war as a primarily psychological reality. That is ironic in light of the massive physical preparations that modern war required and the even more massive physical effects that are its logical outcome. Yet the goal of war preparations is not primarily physical victory but rather psychological intimidation.

Nuclear weapons have changed war not primarily because of their overkill potential. Great powers have always had the potential to massacre the inhabitants of lesser powers and have frequently done so.

The primary novelties in modern war are created by changed relationships between the opponents and between each opponent and the events that would take place before, after and during a war. One change is in the *speed* of destruction possible. Rosecrance observes that,

> History may suggest that increases in the speed of mobilization have also tended to foreshorten the process of political decision-making and this could mean that wars may begin before political solutions of the points at issue can be fully explored.[5]

Mobilization used to take days, weeks even months. During this period hasty decisions could be rethought and further negotiation take place. Once war began it took arduous effort, great cost and usually considerable time to wreak much damage on the enemy. Nuclear weapons are not only fast, they make incredible damage relatively cheap and easy. A missile fired from a submarine or from Europe can destroy Moscow in 15-20 minutes. There is no time for second thoughts.

In the past it took great effort, ingenuity, and sustained cruelty to massacre many defenseless people. Today it can be completed with virtually no effort in just a few minutes. Schelling suggests that you can kill as many people with bayonets as you can with nuclear bombs but few would have the stomach, time, or resources to do so.[6]

There used to be very little political or material purpose in indiscriminate destruction of people. Today, with warfare dependent on the cooperation of whole societies, massacres may be effective politics. The targets of the Hiroshima and

Nagasaki bombs were not the victims but the survivors in Tokyo.

An important qualification to the speed of nuclear war is that a fast war is not a necessary result of nuclear technology but only a possible one.

> That nuclear weapons make it possible to compress the fury of global war into a few hours does not mean that they make it inevitable.[7]

A war between the superpowers could theoretically last over a long period of time and include a gradual escalation and deescalation of nuclear forces before coming to a halt.

Such a limited war would illustrate the psychological and bargaining character of war. In the past only the victor could punish the loser; now both sides are vulnerable. Even in defeat the loser would have the power to destroy its enemy. Thus,

> There was a time when the assurance of victory—false or genuine assurance—could make rational leaders not just willing, but sometimes enthusiastic about war. Not now.[8]

It is possible and perhaps even likely that in a nuclear war a nation might become too weak to survive before its armed forces were even close to defeat. Schelling summarizes the change in war as follows:

> Nuclear weapons can change the speed of events, the control of events, the sequence of events, the relation of victor to vanquished and the relation of homeland to fighting front....It is not overkill that is new; the American army surely had enough 30 caliber bullets to kill everybody in the world in 1945....What is new is plain 'Kill'—the idea that major war might be just a contest in the killing of countries, or not even a contest but just two parallel exercises in devastation.[9]

Finally, the nature of war has been changed by the possibility that even a limited nuclear exchange might threaten the survival of both the "winner", and millions of people in countries outside the conflict. Recent, widely accepted scientific studies have shown that even a modest, "pure" counterforce exchange in which no urban or industrial sites were targeted, surface temperatures all over the Northern Hemisphere would be significantly lowered for at least a year. According to Carl Sagan,

> The pyrotoxins, low light levels, radioactive fallout, subsequent ultraviolet light, and especially the cold are together likely to destroy about all of Northern Hemisphere agriculture, even for the more modest cases... [10]

Millions of people all over the world would starve. Sagan suggests that a major nuclear exchange could threaten the survival of the human species.

The Power of Nuclear Weapons

Bernard Brodie, writing in 1946, prophetically said, "Everything about the Bomb is overshadowed by the twin facts that it exists and that its destructive power is fantastically great."[11] The bomb that Brodie spoke about was the atom bomb. Yet the power of the atom bomb is small in comparison to the potential destructive power of hydrogen weapons. As Churchill said,

> There is an immense gulf between the atomic and the hydrogen bomb. The atomic bomb with all its terror did not carry us outside the scope of human control or manageable events in thought or action, in peace or war. But with the hydrogen bomb, the entire foundation of human affairs was revolutionized.[12]

Some scholars believe the atom bomb could be conceived of as simply a further refinement in the evolution of explosives.[13] It is simply not possible to picture thermonuclear weapons as another step on a ladder. Compared to the ladder they are on the moon!

The atom bomb at Nagasaki was a plutonium-implosion weapon. It derived its power from the fission of an atom. Thermonuclear hydrogen bombs are *triggered* by a uranium or plutonium fission bomb which provides the heat and pressure to set off a thermonuclear reaction in which the nuclei of hydrogen atoms are fused together. In most weapons a third stage of fission is also achieved: fission-fusion- fission. With the H-bomb it is theoretically possible to create a chain reaction of explosions that would be literally unlimited.

> If you fill a ship with U238, (a cheap uranium isotope), and put an H-bomb in the middle of it and blow the whole ship up there would be no limit to the explosion you could get with a thermonuclear reaction.[14]

A 20-megaton thermonuclear bomb is more than a thousand times more powerful than the Nagasaki bomb. If all the explosive power of all the bombs dropped in World War II, including the two atom bombs, were added together, the sum would equal one twelfth of the power of one 20 megaton H-bomb. There is no rationally or morally conceivable use for such a weapon.

The incomprehensible power of nuclear bombs has provoked a change in the *mythologies* and *images* of war that reside in popular literature and imagination. The mythic image of the heroic warrior who wins over impossible odds to victory is no less popular, but is relegated more and more to fantasy and history. Ira Chernus suggests that the thought of nuclear war evokes two major, popular myths.[15] One he calls the " myth of the heroic survivor". Numerous novels portray the new Adam and Eve struggling to build a new world. While they face many difficulties they nevertheless succeed in building an attractive new life. Chernus suggests that this myth reflects the eternal desire to live in a new, fresh cosmos, cleansed of the accumulated "sins" of past history, and the desire for a new beginning...We might well speak there of a new "big bang" which starts the adventure of human life—and of life itself—all over again, with a chance to avoid the mistakes of the past.[16]

The other myth Chernus suggests is myth of no survivors. "In one awful moment, in one big 'whoosh,' everything is destroyed."[17]

Nuclear war is thought of as the end of everything. A myth of total extinction shields us from the likely reality of nuclear war by offering the prospect of a clean and painless end in which all suffering and tension is wiped away in a transcendent experience of total destruction.

Both of these myths are based on denial or ignorance of the empirical realities that would follow nuclear war. Even in the extreme case of an all-out nuclear attack, most of the U.S. population would probably survive the initial blasts and between 30 and 65% would survive the first month.[18] Most of those who did die would face a slow and painful death without medical care. Survivors would face a brutal struggle to maintain a subsistence level of existence. Millions of survivors would be injured and most would eventually die from lack of medical care. Additional millions would starve or freeze during the following, protracted winter. The situation would undoubtedly elicit some acts of heroism but could hardly be thought of as a "clean slate."

The change in war is not that suddenly it is synonymous with the end of history. Once a nuclear war begins it is just as "likely" to end short of an all-out orgy of destruction as it is to proceed to its extreme. Those who speak of winning a "limited" nuclear war base their calculations on as much blindness as those who speak of an inevitable "Armageddon." To assume that nuclear war is the same as any major war only a little bit worse is as myopic and certainly more dangerous than to see nuclear war as the end of all things. The myth of a winnable nuclear war is dangerously common among nuclear strategists.

Many government reports have attempted to gauge the effects of the use of nuclear weapons. Even if only the immediate physical effects of a bomb are considered, there is a huge uncertainty as to what the extent of the damage would be. Military planners and strategists have, in general, estimated the destruction on the conservative side simply because comparatively little is known. A report to Congress from the Office of Technology Assessment reached the conclusion that,

> The effects of a nuclear war that cannot be calculated are at least as important as those for which calculations are attempted. Moreover, even these limited calculations are

subject to very large uncertainties.[19]

Military calculations tend to exclude that which cannot be calculated, (such as deaths by fire damage or starvation), even when such effects are likely to be considerable. Uncertainties result from the necessity of making assumptions about the time of day, time of year, wind, weather, size of bombs (nuclear weapons are impossible to calibrate precisely), exact location of detonations, location of people, how much advance warning, etc.[20]

Nevertheless it is possible to get, if not comprehend, a general idea of some of the immediate effects of a single bomb on a single city. If a single twenty megaton weapon was detonated in New York City the following immediate effects have been calculated:

> Seven million people would die from blast, firestorm and radiation. The blast would cover a radius of ten miles. It would dig a crater 650 feet deep and a mile and a half across even if it was dropped in solid rock. All living things, even in the subways would die...Above the blast a ball of fire would form...four miles wide... (and) eight times hotter than the sun... Two hundred and fifty miles away, as far as Washington, many people would suffer severe eye damage. Within a 39 mile radius a sea of fire would roll and boil fanned by winds of the shock wave. Asphalt, which we do not generally consider combustible, would pass its combustion point of 800 degrees and burn. From the huge cavern dug by the blast, vaporized material pulled up into the air by the fireball would form a radio-active cloud of death...[21]

Detailed studies which examine some of the long term effects of various types of attacks have also been made.[22] But absolutely no one knows what a nuclear war would be like.

Many of the physical effects of nuclear weapons have been discovered by chance, leaving one to wonder what effects remain undiscovered. A U.S. Arms Control and Disarmament Agency paper reported that,

> Another unexpected effect of high altitude bursts was the blackout of high-frequency radio communications.

Disruption of the atmosphere...by nuclear bursts over
the Pacific has wiped out long-distance radio
communications for hours at distances of up to 600 miles
from the burst point. Yet another surprise was the
discovery that electro-magnetic pulses can play havoc
with electrical equipment itself, including some in
command systems that control the nuclear arms
themselves. Much of our knowledge was thus gained by
chance—a fact which should imbue us with humility, as
we contemplate the remaining uncertainties (as well as
the certainties) about nuclear warfare.[23]

The long term ecological impact of a major nuclear conflict
is another area of uncertainty. Controversy surrounds some
estimates of significant damage of the ozone layer of the
earth. Estimates state that if 10% of the U.S. and Soviet
nuclear weapons were detonated, the ozone layer would be
sufficiently diminished to cause blindness to all mammals on
the earth who did not wear protective eye coverings.

Synergistic effects of nuclear war are impossible to
calculate. For example, "...would radiation deaths of birds
and the destruction of insecticide factories have a synergistic
effect?"[24] Insects are far more resistant to radiation than
mammals and might multiply rapidly in the absence of
natural enemies.

It is clear that the impact of even a "small" or "limited"
nuclear attack on the United States would be enormous and
beyond anything ever experienced in American history. A
counter-force attack in which populations were not targeted
could still bring up to 20 million deaths in the short term and
unknown long term effects.[25]

From an economic point of view, and possibly from a
political and social viewpoint as well, conditions after an
attack would get worse before they started to get better.[26]

With the various means of production destroyed, the
survivors would be engaged in a race to produce as much as
they consumed in basic necessities before existing supplies ran
out. Failure to do so could produce more fatalities than the
actual nuclear explosions. The psychological, social, political
and spiritual impact of nuclear war is beyond calculation.

However it is unlikely that the political and social institutions which characterize modern western culture would survive a major nuclear conflict. In even a limited nuclear war, it is difficult to conceive of what "victory" could really mean. Yet both the Soviet Union and the United States are planning for victory, in the sense of a superior ability to recover, if the fatal exchange should ever take place.

A final point to make concerning the power of nuclear weapons has to do with numbers. In the last ten years there has been a dramatic increase in the number and accuracy of nuclear warheads. Corresponding to this increase has been a decrease in megatons and a slight decline in numbers of delivery vehicles. Samuel Huntington and Albert Wohlstetter argue that the results of a qualitative "arms race" may actually be positive.[27] This sanguine viewpoint can only be maintained if one concentrates mainly on Soviet-U.S. balance, controllability of weapons and megatonage. If one focuses on assured destruction capability and likely population fatalities the picture is very grim.

It is warheads that destroy life. With increased numbers and accuracy, megatonage does not measure destruction. Four one megaton bombs blanketed on a city could cause as much immediate destruction and carnage as one 20 megaton weapon, even though the four bombs amount to only four megatons.[28]

Strategists argue that power should only be measured in reliable warheads which could survive a first strike attack by the Soviet Union. Here too there are many uncertainties involved. By manipulating the assumptions and the variables, a large number of different conclusions can be reached. For example, in a Defense Department study of how many U.S. bombers would survive an all-out Soviet counterforce attack there were fourteen different variables.[29] One such variable was how fast would U.S. planes get off the ground. Sixty seconds make a huge difference in the outcome. Depending on the arbitrary choice of numbers, anywhere from one to all of the bombers might survive! Military planners like to assume the worst possible case. The most conservative estimates conclude that, "In military terms, American forces will continue to possess an undisputed assured destruction capacity against the Soviet industrial-civilian complex..."[30]

The United States presently has more than 9,200 strategic nuclear warheads of which about 26 percent are on bombers, 24 percent on land-based missiles and 50 percent on submarines.[31] Most submarines at sea are, at present and for the foreseeable future, invulnerable. Under the worst possible conditions for the U.S., with everything going wrong, a perfectly synchronized, Soviet, all-out, surprise attack would leave at least 3,500 U.S. warheads untouched.[32]

Not counted in this analysis are over 20,000 tactical nuclear weapons. The Soviet Union has over 6,500 strategic bombs which represent a quadrupling of Soviet warheads since 1969.[33] With the likely increase in independently targeted warheads on Soviet missiles and the addition of the Trident and MX missiles to the U.S. armory, the numbers of nuclear weapons in the world is likely to take another huge jump in the next decade.

The inevitable by-product of more missiles is the addition of targets. Even at present levels, a limited conflict in which populations were never targeted would kill several times the number of Americans than were killed in all the combined wars of U.S. history. As the number of warheads increases the likely population fatalities of any conflict continue to rise, along with untold other consequences.

Deterrence: a Strategy of Risks

Deterrence through the threat of retaliation is not a new phenomenon. It has, in one form or another, always been a feature of interstate relations. Deterrence is the power to hurt one's opponent. The purest form of the power to hurt is the taking of hostages. Thomas Schelling's brilliant book on the change in strategy brought about by nuclear weapons, points out the essential difference between strength and violence.

> With strength they can dispute objects of value; with sheer violence they can destroy them. And brute force succeeds when it is used, whereas the power to hurt is most successful when held in reserve.[34]

In modern war the power to hurt has been elevated to the center stage of military strategy. Modern deterrence involves the mutual holding of whole populations hostage. In both world wars the emphasis was on the trial of strength; military victory was the goal. With the rise of nuclear weapons, war as a trial of strength is no longer possible. War has become a process of bargaining rather than an alternative to bargaining. As Schelling says,

> War appears to be, or threatens to be, not so much a contest of strength as one of endurance, nerve, obstinacy and pain... not so much a contest of military strength as a bargaining process—dirty, extortionate and often quite reluctant..."[35]

There are some inherent and deadly paradoxes to the strategy of deterrence. One is that war is deterred by the manipulation of risks. Assuming that no rational party wants nuclear war, the paradox of deterrence is that the danger of war is held off by the threat of war. Risks are deterred with risks. The greater the risk the more effective the deterrent. Threats to use nuclear weapons entail great risks because if the threat does not achieve its desired result, the threatener will have to carry out the threat or lose credibility.

For deterrence to work the threat must be persuasive. An opponent is not likely to heed a threat intended to halt aggression if it appears likely that the threatener will back down rather than risk war. On the other hand, if the enemy can be convinced that you cannot or will not back down, deterrence can be very effective.

> If you burn your bridges so that you cannot retreat, your enemy has new calculations to make because he knows you can't do what you might prefer.[36]

Commitment increases the strength of deterrence through the process of surrendering and destroying options. A doomsday machine that would blow up the whole world would provide an excellent deterrent to aggression only if it could be rigged to go off automatically and necessarily in the event of aggression. Otherwise it would be ineffectual. The effectiveness of the deterrent is directly related to the level and plausibility of danger it provokes.

One way to make a deterrent threat persuasive is to cultivate an image of insanity or fanaticism. According to H.R. Haldeman, Nixon understood this and attempted to use it to end the Vietnam war. Haldeman reports that Nixon said,

> I call it the madman theory, Bob. I want the North Vietnamese to believe I've reached the point where I might do any—that, "for God's sake, you know Nixon is obsessed about Communism—and he has his hand on the nuclear button"—and Ho Chi Minh himself will be in Paris in two days begging for peace.[37]

Nixon's threats were not effective because the North Vietnamese knew that U.S. opinion had turned against the war and that an elected president would have to pull out sooner or later.

Strategically, deterrence can be considered in three categories: 1. deterrence of a direct attack on the U.S., 2. extended deterrence to prevent attacks on allies and friends, and 3. the interaction between deterrence and "compellance." These three are listed in order of difficulty. When the U.S. enjoyed a virtual monopoly in nuclear armaments during the fifties, the strategy of massive retaliation tended to lump these three together.

Deterrence was officially proclaimed the first principle of strategy in 1953. Any Soviet aggression anywhere was threatened with nuclear retaliation. The threat had some degree of credibility because the Soviets did not have the power to respond in kind. A major way in which President Eisenhower was able to bring the Korean war to a close was through a secret threat to use nuclear bombs.[38] Massive retaliation was understood to mean the targeting and obliteration of whole cities.

As the Soviet Union gained nuclear strength, massive retaliation gave way to mutually assured destruction (M.A.D.). Threats could not be made with impunity when the major opponent also had nuclear weapons. While American presidents continued to flex their nuclear muscles with threats intended to compel obedience, the threats were not particularly successful.[39]

In the eyes of the American public and as a basic minimum of deterrence, M.A.D. has remained central to American strategy ever since. M.A.D. has never been a doctrine that could arouse much enthusiasm. The idea of "city-swapping" and "spasm" warfare seems too fatalistic. For military planners, M.A.D. seemed to spell the end of rational warfare.

On June 16, 1962, Robert McNamara announced a major shift in U.S. policy which provoked much controversy. McNamara's speech announced publicly a concept of *counterforce nuclear warfare* which had been a covert part of U.S. strategy for some time. He said,

> Principal military objectives, in the event of a nuclear war stemming from a major attack on the alliance, should be the destruction of the enemy's military forces, not of his civilian population.[40]

McNamara explained his policy as a return to approaching nuclear conflict in "much the same way that more conventional military operations have been regarded in the past."[41] McNamara's counterforce strategy, also called the "no-cities doctrine," included the idea of destroying the enemy's nuclear forces. Nuclear war was to be avoided if at all possible, but if it broke out it was to be kept "limited."

Like the earlier "massive retaliation," the McNamara/ Kennedy counterforce doctrine made sense in the light of the large lead the U.S. enjoyed in the arms race. With a relatively large nuclear stockpile, the U.S. could realistically hope to limit the damage the Soviets could do by blanketing the few Soviet missiles with nuclear bombs. The Soviet Union did not like the idea as they had no comparable capability. The Soviet Prime Minister termed the plan "monstrous."[42] Counterforce doctrine was widely perceived as very threatening to the Soviets because it suggested the possibility of a U.S. preemptive first strike.

McNamara strongly repudiated any attempt to achieve a counterforce capability that would make a first strike possible. Nevertheless as Soviet missiles became targets the rationale was laid for an arms race of much greater proportions. The U.S. already had an overwhelming, invulnerable ability to destroy all the large cities in the U.S.S.R.. Of course the wild card in a "limited war" counterforce strategy is the danger of escalation. An early critic predicted,

> It would quickly expand into a war against cities and people. Because many cities are close to missile bases and airfields, it has been estimated that some 30 million Americans would be killed in a first, counterforce-type strike. The first bombs to fall would knock out most communications and reconnaissance facilities. Neither government would know whether the other was "playing the game," which forces were still in existence, and what its own men were doing. In such confusion, total war would be almost inescapable.[43]

In spite of concerns from many quarters, the die was cast. Counterforce planning has been central to U.S. nuclear strategy ever since. As Mandelbaum put it,

> ...although his three successors differed from John Kennedy in both personal and political terms, all three followed the broad outlines of policies, for nuclear weapons, that he and Robert McNamara had established.[44]

Jimmy Carter and Ronald Reagan have also continued to emphasize counterforce capability. One change has been a relaxation of the concern McNamara showed about avoiding any impression of attaining a first strike capability. First strike capability is to be distinguished from first use. No American president has renounced the "right" to use nuclear weapons first.

A first strike option opens up many dangers because it intensifies the advantages of launching one's own weapons first, before an opponent destroys them. A really effective first strike capability might once again make it possible to "win" a nuclear war, at least in terms of immediate relative damage. The possibility of severe ecological damage would make such a victory short-lived.

McNamara later backed off from the emphasis on counterforce contained in the Ann Arbor speech because, according to a close associate, he saw "that it was confusing the far more important message that nobody wins a nuclear war."[45] In fact, Senator Hubert Humphrey reported that McNamara,

> ...ended his long tour in the Defense Department convinced that the most dangerous thing in the world is a state of mind—the belief among powerful men on both sides, in the face of all the horrendous evidence to the contrary, that somehow the scientists will yet find a way to employ nuclear weapons so that military men may again win a war.[46]

In 1974, Secretary of Defense James R. Schlesinger announced a "new strategic targeting doctrine" that was, in fact, just a reiteration of the counterforce policy announced by McNamara.[47] This was repeated by Harold Brown in the Carter Administration who said:

> It has never been U.S. policy to limit ourselves to massive counter-city operations in retaliation...For nearly 20 years we have explicitly included a range of employment option...In particular we have always considered it important in the event of war to be able to attack the forces that could do damage to the U.S. and its allies.[48]

The only new element in this strategy was the increased public exposure of the doctrine. The American public continues to think about deterrence in M.A.D. terms.

Some analysts believe that the U.S. had gone beyond limited counterforce policy and is now moving toward a first strike capability. Nuclear strategist Alain Enthoven called such a strategy dangerous and futile:

> dangerous because increasing the enemy's perceived vulnerability of his forces might put pressure on him to launch those forces in a crisis before they are destroyed on the ground; futile because even the ability to destroy all the Soviet silos would leave hundreds of their submarine launched missiles at sea able to destroy our society many times over.[49]

Futile or not, former Lockheed missile designer, Robert C.

Aldridge argued in 1979 that the purpose of present U.S. weapons technology points towards a first strike. Aldridge analyzes a first strike capability in terms of five elements:

> 1.) a space warfare ability to destroy enemy early warning and communications satellites, 2.) extremely accurate missiles and bombers to destroy the opponent's missile silos and other land targets, 3.) an anti-submarine warfare force able to sink hostile missile-launching subs, 4.) a ballistic missile and bomber defense capable of intercepting any surviving enemy missiles or aircraft that are launched in retaliation and 5.) an intricate network of command, control and communication to coordinate and integrate 1) through 4).[50]

With the apparent invulnerability of nuclear submarines and the impediments of the Anti-Ballistic Missile treaty, it would seem that first strike capabilities are not yet a reality. Experts continue to maintain that in spite of rapid, overall increases in the effectiveness of anti-submarine warfare, (A.S.W) there is little likelihood of achieving a confident submarine "kill-capability" in the near future.[51] It is one thing to be able to track a submarine and another to destroy it before it could fire its missiles.

Aldridge argues that the relatively small number of Soviet nuclear submarines away from port at one time, (around 10 at the present), makes anti-submarine warfare an effective possibility.[52] Aldridge also foresaw the current debate about the possibility of missile defense systems. He argued that "Homing Interceptor Technology" and "Directed Energy Weapons" are top secret technological advances which may greatly increase the effectiveness of A.B.M. systems if the A.B.M. treaty is not renewed.[53]

Aldridge's concerns, written in 1979, are given further credence by the now public debate over the Strategic Defense Initiative (S.D.I.). On March 23, 1983 President Reagan announced in a nationally televised speech, "a comprehensive and intensive effort to define a long-term research and development program to begin to achieve our ultimate goal of eliminating the threat posed by strategic nuclear missiles." The plan was promptly labeled "Star Wars" by the press.

The star wars controversy revises many arguments that have been heard before in the ABM debates of 1967-72. The major difference lies in the improved technology proposed by S.D.I. and the extravagant claims of the President. The basic idea of S.D.I. is that strategic missiles would be shot down from space before they could do any damage. President Reagan asked in his speech,

What if free people could live secure in the knowledge that their security did not rest upon the threat of instant U.S. retaliation to deter a Soviet attack that we could intercept and destroy strategic ballistic missiles before they reached our own soil or that of our allies?[54]

Intercontinental ballistic missiles (ICBMs) go through four phases: boost phase, post-boost phase, midcourse phase and terminal phase. During the 1950s and 1960s, ballistic missile defenses (BMDs) concentrated on the last two phases since attacking the missiles from space seemed unfeasible. S.D.I. plans call for intercepting missiles in all four phases with special attention to the boost phase. A boost phase "kill" is especially attractive because an entire busload of warheads and decoys would be destroyed by hitting a single missile.

S.D.I. has stirred intense debate and severe criticism from the scientific community. Very few technical experts believe that a comprehensive "astrodome" population defense as envisaged by the President is possible. In a Background Paper for the Office of Technological Assessment and the U.S. Congress, Ashton B. Carter concludes:

The prospect that emerging "Star Wars" technologies, when further developed, will provide a perfect or near-perfect defense system, literally removing from the hands of the Soviet Union the ability to do socially mortal damage to the United States with nuclear weapons, is so remote that it should not serve as the basis of public expectation or national policy... This judgement appears to be the consensus among informed members of the defense technical community... Mutually Assumed Destruction (M.A.D.)... is likely to persist for the foreseeable future.[55]

Likewise, former Defense Secretaries Harold Brown and James Schlesinger have both warned that there is no possibility that ballistic defense systems could protect our populations.[56]

The seriousness of the criticisms from the scientific community have persuaded most informed S.D.I. supporters to retreat from advocating a comprehensive rational defense. The debate has now shifted to the possible advantages of a limited B.M.D. that would give our population marginal or even no protection. Only selected military or governmental targets would be protected. Stephen Van Evera comments that,

> Such limited defenses are now the only variety that are seriously discussed by most military scientists and defense experts....Nevertheless, President Reagan still endorses his original aim...and the public debate largely proceeds as if an impermeable "Astrodome" defense remains the official aim of S.D.I.

The result is a

> surreal public dialogue focused on the merits and drawbacks of a Star Wars I "Astrodome" defense that defense professionals dismissed long ago...[57]

The public justification of "Star Wars", that it delivers us from deterrence and the moral dilemmas of M.A.D., is false and misleading. At least in the eyes of the Soviets, "Star Wars" is a potential addition to U.S. offensive capability. Not only will it invalidate the A.B.M. treaty, it would also be a potent contribution to a first-strike capability. S.D.I. provides the impetus for a huge and costly leap in the arms race by threatening the deterrent capability of the Soviet Union.

It is not my purpose to evaluate the many nuances in the debate over S.D.I., only to show that it does not affect the basic structure of M.A.D. as a technological reality. U.S. strategy has progressed well beyond the concept of "finite deterrence" as it was defined by two of McNamara's top systems analysts:

Once we are sure that, in retaliation, we can destroy the
Soviet Union and other potential attackers as modern
societies, we cannot increase our security or power against
them by threatening to destroy more.[58]

There are deep moral problems with each of the strategic
policies that the United States has adopted. The early policy
of massive retaliation made the dubious assumption that the
United States had a right to threaten apocalyptic doom on
any nation whose government was guilty of aggression. While
restraint was used in the application of this threat, the threat
itself presumed a self- righteousness that virtually placed the
U.S. government in the position of God. The idea that any
government could ever have the right to rain nuclear
destruction on another people, for any reason, is morally
abhorrent.

Mutually assured destruction, while provoked by necessity,
at least has the virtue of an ambiguous intention to prevent
both sides from using their weapons. Yet from an absolute
moral perspective, M.A.D. has the same defect as massive
retaliation. It assumes that an acceptable defense against
massacre is to threaten massacre. Moreover the threat implies
that a legitimate response to the murder of our defenseless
population is to murder another defenseless population.

Counterforce strategy has the apparent moral advantage of
maintaining deterrence without targeting populations.
However, counterforce has never been completely separated
from M.A.D. in strategy. Counterforce does not remove the
threat to populations but supplements it in hopes of avoiding
the extremes of all-out destruction. Five additional points
undermine the counterforce claim to moral legitimacy.

First, the tremendous "collateral damage" to civilian
populations and the ecosystem that would accompany
counterforce nuclear warfare undermines the claim that
populations would not be targeted. Second, counterforce
warfare initiates a scale of conflict that would be very hard to
manage. Escalation to all-out warfare would be a distinct
possibility. Third, preparation for counterforce nuclear
conflict undermines deterrence by encouraging the illusion that

relative nuclear "victory" is possible through rationally limited warfare. Fourth, counterforce preparations raise the fear of an enemy first strike and stimulate the immoral hope of achieving a first strike. And finally counterforce policy gives rise to a costly arms race that diverts precious resources from urgent social needs.

A first strike nuclear strategy raises all of the moral objections of all of the above strategies combined. It is a moral and practical nightmare that no responsible political leader would admit to publicly. In his speech of March 23, 1983, President Reagan denied that S.D.I. had any aggressive intent. But Van Evera indicates a first-strike capability is at least a muted part of the "Star Wars" debate. He says,

> Finally, expressing a little discussed but important argument for limited defenses, some advocates suggest that a thin population defense, if married to American first-strike counterforce weapons (such as MX ICBM and the Trident D5 SLBM), can give the United States a meaningful first-strike counterforce capability against the Soviet Union. Defense would thus restore American superiority, re-establish the credibility of American nuclear threats and extend American deterrence over Europe and other areas.[59]

One of the results of an increasing emphasis on counterforce capabilities is an increasing number of nuclear warheads. Every major military target requires a missile (usually two or three missiles).

The frequent moral objections that have been raised against the increasing number of nuclear weapons, prompted the legitimate response that more bombs do not *necessarily* increase the likelihood of war. A country that has a comfortable margin of safety against a first-strike may be less tempted to begin a preemptive attack.

Large numbers of missiles also have the beneficial effect of increasing the "withhold capability," of a country under attack. In the event of a first strike against a country with many weapons there would not be as great a temptation to launch an immediate massive response. Weapons could be withheld without the fear that they would all be destroyed.

This flexibility, along with increased accuracy and decreased megatonage, increases the control that can be exercised over nuclear war. Unfortunately it also decreases the deterrent to both sides. "Limited" nuclear conflict becomes a conceivable option.

In recent years, the official confidence in the Pentagon that small conflicts can be kept small and that limited nuclear war can be kept limited has risen sharply. The former assumption that any nuclear war would quickly escalate to city swapping has been replaced.

Part of the reason for this confidence is the experience of Korea and Vietnam, both of which were serious East-West conflicts in which nuclear exchanges were avoided. It was shown that no sane person could make a rational political decision to initiate a large nuclear exchange.

Deterrence and Rationality

The problem with the above line of reasoning is that it assumes rational people in full control of events. Schelling points out that because there is no rationally foreseeable route by which the Soviet Union and the United States could engage in a major nuclear war does not imply that one could not happen.

> It only means that if it does occur it will result from a process that is not entirely foreseen from reactions that are not fully predictable, from decisions that are not wholly deliberate, from events that are not fully under control.[60]

John Steinbrunner comments on the irony of Western leaders' assumptions of completely rational processes in the light of the actions of the Kaiser in World War I and Hitler in World War II.[61] According to Steinbrunner, deterrence strategy rests on,

> the truly heroic assumption, that the behavior of very large modern governments...will approximate the behavior of rationally calculating individual players in the simple, prototype game.[62]

Strategic thinking assumes a kind of rationality which has little precedent in wartime history. Deterrent strategy seeks larger and larger margins of guaranteed destruction in order to reinforce its own logic in the face of possible miscalculation or irrationality by the enemy. Steinbrunner calculates that 10% of U.S. strategic forces would provide a more than adequate rational deterrent, in which case 90% of U.S. strategic forces are provided as a hedge against errors in the rational decision process.

An anomaly in deterrence strategy, based on either massive retaliation or counterforce, is that in the event of an all-out first strike, there would remain no rational purpose for retaliation. Thus,

> If simple, direct and perfect rationality existed on both sides of the strategic confrontation, this paradox of the retaliatory threat would presumably lead to a preemptive, counterforce attack by the first side truly understanding the conundrum.[63]

Clearly no such simple rationality exists. Whoever launched the holocaust of a first strike could not count on the controlled rationality of the surviving victims to not strike back, with or without rational purpose. Even if invulnerability could be guaranteed, it is not at all clear that the victor would benefit in the long run from turning a whole continent into a radioactive wasteland. Human beings are not simply rational or irrational, they are also strong or weak and good and evil. A nuclear first strike would be evil. It is hard to imagine anyone not feeling some restraint of conscience before initiating such a holocaust. It is a simple matter to imagine an irrational evil response by the victim of an unprovoked strike.

Steinbrunner rejects the view that stable deterrence depends on the fine details of the technical balance.[64] Simple rational deterrence was achieved long ago and cannot be reinforced by overkill because nuclear war is not likely to occur as a result of rational calculation. Given the enormous complexity of modern government,

> Deterrence in a cybernetic process...is most likely to fail,

not as a result of a technical accident, an unauthorized action or a cold-blooded calculation, but rather as an unintended, unexpected consequence of a limited strategic maneuver.[65]

The more complex and extended the defense establishment, the more difficult it becomes to control the decision processes that control it. When offensive capabilities are geared to an enormous response to aggression, a serious problem arises in limiting the bureaucracy to a moderate response. Increasing the number and capability of strategic forces does not necessarily stabilize deterrence. Steinbrunner argues that,

> The American ability to threaten massive retaliation and actually conduct a limited counterforce response is not very sensitive to substantial force disparities; the hypothetical political effects of those disparities range from very speculative to highly implausible.[66]

Whether or not Steinbrunner is right, (and I think he is), no one seems willing to experiment with what would happen if the U.S. had "inferior" forces to the Soviet Union. The logic of rational decision process which measures power in fighting potential is too firmly entrenched in political life. Yet the costs of such "rationality" continue to skyrocket.

The centrality of deterrence forces a rethinking of the meaning of rationality in security policy. Two levels of deterrence rationality seem to conflict with each other. What is rational if it works is irrational if it does not. Kennedy embodied this dilemma during the Cuban missile crisis. Schelling says,

> The Cuban Crisis was a contest in risk taking, involving steps that would make no sense if they led predictably and ineluctably to a major war, yet would also have made no sense if they were completely without danger.[67]

Can it be rational to deter one evil by threatening to set in motion a greater evil? Deterrent strategy assumes that it is, but the answer seems to lie in its results. If the deterrent succeeds and both evils are averted then the threat seems rational. However if the deterrent fails and the greater evil comes about, the threat seems irrational.

The same conundrum underlies the debate between M.A.D. and counterforce strategies. If the deterrent works then M.A.D. is rational and counterforce is a very expensive and irrational means of reducing the deterrent. If the deterrent breaks down M.A.D. is literally mad while counterforce at least offers the chance of restraint and far less damage. Many able minds have wrestled with this problem and found no solution. The two strategies cannot be reconciled, nor can either be proved superior. Moreover if the deterrent really broke down, unilateral disarmament might appear to have been the most rational possibility.

In relation to nuclear war, rationality is an elusive quality that appears to rest on the perception and calculation of unknown, indeed unknowable events. In some cases, the difference between positions may be based on how the problem is *perceived*—for example, how likely an all-out nuclear war is, or how much likelihood can be tolerated in a given policy. Unfortunately, differences of perception are not usually merely matters of fact that can be settled by reasoned discussion. With an almost infinite number of potentially relevant facts to choose from, probability or improbability assertions are inevitably pleas to pay attention to some facts more than others.

For example, Sidney Lens and Robert Gardiner both consider the likelihood of general nuclear war far past the point of tolerability.[68] They depict the buildup of arms as not only immoral but irrational. In contrast, Frederick Bonkovsky and Kenneth Waltz consider general nuclear war as practically impossible.[69]

Sometimes different positions are held not on the basis of different perceptions of the problem, but different *perceptions* of the solution. Two authors may agree that the likelihood of a nuclear exchange is of unacceptable gravity but may disagree on what is the best way to get out from under this threat. John Bennett is not less concerned about the danger of a nuclear exchange than Robert Drinan, but Bennett rejects unilateral disarmament because, unlike Drinan, he is not convinced that unilateral disarmament is either possible or necessarily likely to reduce the probability of nuclear holocaust.[70]

Anti-war writers sometimes argue that unilateral disarmament would automatically end the danger of nuclear devastation or at least substantially reduce it. Other scholars sometimes assume that any unilateral disarmament would upset the strategic balance and increase the likelihood of nuclear war. The problem is, like nuclear war, nuclear disarmament is an unprecedented event and any confident assertion of its results is a case of special pleading.

The definition of rationality often depends on what different authors perceive to be *acceptable risks.* A 1% risk of nuclear devastation may be a rationally tolerable risk for one and a completely irrational risk to another. There is no way to determine such issues objectively. Furthermore, one person may perceive a 1% risk of escalation to all-out war if nuclear weapons are used at all while another scholar may perceive an 80% risk once the nuclear threshold is crossed. Subjective and inconclusive calculations can easily determine which position one holds.

There is no rational solution to these dilemmas. Bonkovsky suggests a policy scientific approach by which values are assigned according to political factors and decisions are made in accord with mathematically cost/benefit computations.[71] But there is no mathematical formulation for assigning values or computing risks.

Anatol Rapoport suggests that these are fundamental flaws in formally rational modes of analyzing the security dilemma. Rapoport begins by pointing to some ragged edges in strategic decision-making theory such as the common failure to distinguish between formal, prescriptive and descriptive theory. What happens in a model doesn't indicate what should happen nor what will happen. The term "probability" is also problematic in decision theory; "...the term 'probability of a nuclear war' has nothing to do with frequency since nuclear war has not occurred. Therefore 'probability' here means degree of belief."[72] Rapoport argues that,

...although 'facts' can always be marshalled in support of probabilities to be assigned to unique events, we are at liberty to select those facts, and select them we must... In

the last analysis then, arguments in support of
probabilities assigned to events are pleas to pay attention
to some facts more than to others.[73]

How facts and values are weighed is a major issue.
Rapoport suggests that it is impossible to determine a strictly
"rational" decision, given only the material facts of the
situation. Any decision reflects ethical values of some kind.
Rapoport makes his point vivid by discussing the problem of
estimating the value of human life in political *'utiles.'*
Herman Kahn discussed the price Americans would be
willing to pay in order to punish Soviet nuclear Aggression.

If 180 million dead is too high a price to pay... what price
would we be willing to pay? I have discussed this question
with many Americans, and after about fifteen minutes of
discussion their estimates of an acceptable, price,
generally fall between 10 and 60 million, clustering toward
the upper number.[74]

Snyder points out,

Perhaps the most uncertain factor for the U.S. is the degree of
prospective damage which would be sufficient to deter the
U.S.S.R. from attacking. Would the Soviets be deterred by the
prospect of losing ten cities? or two cities? or fifty cities? No
one knows...[75]

Implicit in Rapoport's discussion is the value question of
how to weigh the various ideological components of security,
national interest and democracy against the cost of nuclear
war. Rapoport argues that it is impossible not to weigh them
in determining rational decision making.
Strategic thinking inevitably leads into the 'zero-sum trap'
according to Rapoport, "a closed system of thought in which
the only reality is a struggle between participants with
diametrically opposed interests.[76] Psychological know-how
will not help because the underpinnings of knowledge do not fit
into "unidimensional utile scales." These underpinnings,
Rapoport defines as, "the deep commitments of people, their

concept of equity, their real hierarchies of values, and their noble and ignoble impulses which may invalidate the strategists' entire conceptual system.[77] In neglecting these essentials, Rapoport contends that "the strategist defends nightmare images of the world as a 'realist' vision, forgetting that any image of the world is compounded of elements which one has selected for observation.[78]

The thrust of Rapoport's argument emphasizes the complexity of international relations and the magnitude of unknown factors. Thus it is not a big surprise that in rejecting formal, deductive reasoning he opts for an informal, intuitive approach. He suggests that the problems are too complex to approach in a rational, logical way. "Insights" rather than answers are the result of this approach.

Rapoport points out that the decisive determinants of war and peace are elusive. "...We do not know how and why nations become or cease to be 'aggressive.' We do not know how the actions and wills of millions of people are welded into a war machine."[79] Rapoport implies that we cannot know such things at a rational level at this point in history. He suggests that we need to learn to ask different questions. "These questions may lead to an answer but they may also lead to a new insight, e.g., that the problem is unsolvable and must be reformulated.[80]

Rapoport considers the basic components of the security dilemma to be based on subjective estimates. He presents three basic differences between conscience and strategy-directed thinking.[81] 1) The strategic thinker considers choice of action in terms of impact on the environment while the conscience-directed person thinks in terms of its impact on the actor. 2) The strategist begins only when values (*utiles*) are given or assumed while the conscience-driven thinker considers the determination of those values to be the principle problem. He rejects the notion that values are purely relative. 3) The strategist assumes that the state of the world is an objective fact to be analyzed while the conscience thinker believes that how one analyzes the world and what values are assigned determines to a significant degree what the world is becoming.

Perhaps the most significant difference between Rapoport

and the strategist is their contrasting evaluation of power.

> The critic is convinced of the corrupting effect of power,
> especially unimpeded power...the acceptance of
> international relations as a power game seems
> self-defeating to one who questions the value of power.[82]

The underlying assumption of strategic thinking is that
power is a pure good. It is the goal of strategy. Rapoport
implies that the strategist's "objective" analysis of the "real
world" itself creates and maintains the security dilemma.

Can there be a real dialogue between strategy and
conscience? "... I am not sure", answers Rapoport,

> ...Here I believe is essential incompatibility, not merely a
> result of misunderstanding. I do not believe one can bring
> both into focus. One cannot play chess if one becomes
> aware of the pieces as living souls and of the fact that the
> whites and blacks have more in common with each other
> than with the players. Suddenly one loses all interest in
> who will be the champion.[83]

Rapoport has unveiled the tension that exists between
moral imperatives and the apparently rational dictates of
military defense. In one sense there is no difference between
morality and rationality. Rationality cannot operate without
making moral judgements about what values and goals to seek.
Similarly morality assumes that its values, and its choice of
means to reach its goals, are ultimately rational. So morality
is rational and rationality is moral.

Such an equation is seldom self-evident. Moral policy may
lead to material disaster. Policy that is rationally designed
to maximize material values may appear morally bankrupt.
The difference is that "rationality" traditionally chooses
foreseeable material consequences as its goal while morality
emphasized goals whose values and meaning transcend
foreseeable consequences. Rationality still depends upon
morality because the choice of foreseeable material
consequences is itself a moral one.

One reason politics is often assumed to be "rational" rather
than "moral" is that in a pluralistic context which lacks
consensus on transcendent values, foreseeable material

consequences serve as a lowest common denominator for decision-making. The problem with the application of such rationality to modern defense policy is that no one knows the consequences of the various options. Nuclear weapons have backed us into a corner. Of the available exits, some or all of them may lead to disaster. And there is no way to tell which ones are safer.

In ethical terms, teleological political ethics have brought us to an impasse. When rational calculation reaches its limit and the potential choices have urgent ethical implications, it becomes imperative to listen to deontological modes of thought. It is clear that nuclear weapons cannot be justified in terms of absolute morality. Deontological ethics may not tell us *how* to move politically away from a nuclear defense. But the fact that we must move away is clear.

Unfortunately, political policy makers often find it easier to minimize the moral and physical danger of nuclear weapons rather than to allow ethical concerns to upset entrenched modes of reasoning about defense. In the name of rational analysis of relative capabilities, some military strategists ignore the horrendous destructiveness of even "small" nuclear bombs. It borders on insanity to speak of "surgical strikes" against counterforce targets with 150 to 200 kiloton bombs. The bomb that leveled Hiroshima, massacred its inhabitants and still causes deformities today was "only" approximately 15 kilotons. The result of dropping even one nuclear weapon on one counterforce target would be a stupendous, incalculable event that could change or end history.

Certainly it is no foregone conclusion that conflict between the superpowers would lead to the use of nuclear weapons, or that the use of small nuclear weapons would lead to the use of large nuclear weapons, or that large nuclear bombs would lead to the end of civilization. The possibility may even be remote that such escalation would take place. But rational analysis cannot predict the outcome of events for which there is no precedent.

Conclusion

This chapter has attempted to demonstrate how nuclear weapons have changed the meaning of war. The phrase "meaning of war" may need further explanation. "War" is both an idea and an empirical reality. Thus far, nuclear war is primarily an abstract idea. It has no empirical referent in history. Nuclear weapons and the preparations for nuclear war are concrete realities that are based on the abstract idea of nuclear war. The idea of nuclear war corresponds to an ever possible future event which could eclipse most, if not all of the past events of human history.

The meaning of the idea of nuclear war as well as the understanding of its likely shape are thus of immense importance. How well the meaning of nuclear war is understood may determine whether the idea becomes an empirical reality. Furthermore our understanding exerts a tremendous influence on our present values. The idea of nuclear war has more impact on the present life of U.S. citizens, measured in terms of how they spend their money, than any other single influence.

The first section of this chapter discussed how a nuclear war would differ from wars in the past. Not only the process leading up to war, but war itself would be a process of bargaining by threat. The nature of the war would be circumscribed by the fact that each opponent has the ability to destroy the other, even in defeat.

In the second section, we considered the power of nuclear weapons and the likely effects of nuclear war. Nuclear weapons have qualitatively changed the physical results of war. Even the victor might be destroyed by the ecological damage to the planned.

In the third section, the change in war was described in terms of the strategies that nuclear weapons have elicited. Deterrence and the manipulation of risk have become the central functions of defense policy. The promise of a Star Wars defensive system to deliver us from the insecurity of deterrence has proved illusory. There is no military strategy that can guarantee nuclear security.

The final section focused on rationality in relation to strategy. The need to depend on rationality in nuclear strategy was considered in relation to the great fear of irrationality. In our nuclear age, rationality must seek a closer relation to morality.

There is no single meaning of nuclear war. We seek to comprehend the small number of facts that we know about nuclear war by means of metaphors and analogies. Much thought about war today is dependent on a historical stream of ideas, images and metaphors that have been developed over the centuries in response to the phenomenon of war. In the next two chapters, we will critically evaluate the way in which just war theory and political realism respond to changes in the meaning of war.

1   Carl Von Clausewitz, *On War*, Michael Howard and Peter Paret, eds. & trans. (Princeton, NJ: Princeton University Press, 1976), p. 89.

2   Ibid., pp. 79, 120 and 357. cf. Michael Mandelbaum, *The Nuclear Question* (New York: Cambridge University Press, 1979), pp. 9ff.

3   Bernard Brodie, ed., *The Absolute Weapon: Atomic Power and World Order* (New York : Harcourt Brace, 1946) p. 76.

4   Thomas C. Schelling, *Arms and Influence* (New Haven, Conn.: Yale University Press, 1966), p. 2.

5   Richard N. Rosecrance, *Action and Reaction in World Politics* (Boston: Little, Brown and Co., 1963), p. 287.

6   Schelling, p. 321.

7   Ibid., p. 20.

8   Ibid., p. 22.

9   Ibid., p. 23.

10 Carl Sagan, "Nuclear War and Climatic Catastrophe" in *The Long Darkness*, Lester Grimspoon, ed. (New Haven: Yale University Press, 1986), p. 30.

11 Brodie, p. 51.

12 Quoted in Norman Moss, *Men Who Play God* (New York: Harper and Row, 1968), p. 51.

13 See Mandelbaum, p. 49.

14 Daniel Ellsberg, "Nuclear Armament" (Berkeley, CA: Conservation Press, 1980), p. 7.

15 Ira Chernus, "Mythologies of Nuclear War," unpublished paper presented at the American Academy of Religion Meeting, San Francisco, December 19-21, 1981. Chernus draws heavily on the work of Robert Lifton.

16 Ibid., pp. 4-5.

17 Ibid., p. 10.

18 Office of Technology Assessment (O.T.A.) , *The Effects of Nuclear War* (Washington, D.C.: Congress of the United States, 1980), p. 18.

19 Ibid., p. 7.

20 Ibid., p. 23.

21 These calculations are drawn from governmental studies of American test blasts and through measurements of the two atomic bombs in Japan. They are compiled in Thomas Stonier, *Nuclear Disaster*.

22 For example, see Committee on Banking, Housing and Urban Affairs, *Economic and Social Consequences of Nuclear Attacks on the United States*, A study prepared for the Joint Committee on Defense Production, Congress of the United States,

Washington D.C. : U.S. Government Printing Office, 1979. Many studies have resulted from the "nuclear winter" debate. For some responses and many references see Grinspoon, ed., *The Long Darkness.*

23 U.S. Arms Control and Disarmament Agency, *Worldwide Effects on Nuclear War: Some Perspectives,* report no. 81 Washington D.C. : U.S. Government Printing Office, 1975, p. 5.

24 *The Effects of Nuclear War,* (O.T.A report), p. 245.

25 Ibid., p. 9.

26 Ibid., p. 11.

27 Samuel Huntington, "Arms Races: Prerequisites and Results" *Public Policy,* 8 (1958), pp. 41-86 and Albert Wohlstetter, "Is There a Strategic Arms Race?" *Foreign Policy,* No. 15 (Summer, 1974).

28 This applies only to immediate casualties. Long term ecological effects such as damage to the ozone layer and long distance effects such as the spread of radiation might be more severe with a larger bomb. Such effects cannot be accurately predicted and are often hardly mentioned in government reports. Jonathan Schell's discussion of human "extinction" is based on an extremely pessimistic view of the unpredictable effects of an "all- out" nuclear war.

29 Reported by Wallace J. Theis, Political Science 228A, "American National Security Policy", Winter, 1981, University of California, Berkeley, CA.

30 Richard Burt, "Reassessing the Strategic Balance," *International Security,* 5, No. 1 (Summer, 1980), p. 43.

31 Harold Brown, *Annual Department of Defense Report, Fiscal Year, 1981,* Washington D.C., p. 89.

32 Hatfield Background Report, "The Age of Anxiety: Emerging Nuclear Tensions in the 1980's," Report for Senator Mark O. Hatfield, No. 193 (Washington D.C., June, 1981). Actually the Defense Department estimates 4-5,000.

33 Brown, p. 89.

34 Schelling, p. 3.

35 Ibid., p. 7.

36 Ibid., p. 42.

37 Harry R. Haldeman, with Joseph Di Mono, *The Ends of Power* (New York: Times Books, 1978), p. 83.

38 Dwight D. Eisenhower, *Mandate for Change,* 1953-1956 (New York: Doubleday, 1963), pp. 178-81.

See also Alexander L. George and Richard Smoke, *Deterrence in American Foreign Policy,* (New York: Columbia University Press 1974), pp. 237-41. The following is only the briefest outline of U.S.

nuclear strategy. For more detailed information see, Jerome H. Kahn, *Security in the Nuclear Age* (Washington D.C.: The Brookings Institution, 1975), and Michael Mandelbaum, *The Nuclear Question* (New York: Cambridge University Press, 1979).

39 See Daniel Ellsberg, "Nuclear Armament," p. 4 for a documented list of American nuclear threats that include threats by every president from Truman through Nixon.

40 McNamara's speech is reprinted in Richard Stebbens, ed., *Documents and American Foreign Relations, 1962* (New York: Harper and Row, 1963), p. 233.

41 Ibid.,p. 232. This statement is embarrassingly mistaken. Counterforce nuclear war is not strategically similar to conventional war.

42 William V. O'Brian, "The Fate of Counterforce," *The Commonweal*, May 17, 1963, p. 218.

43 James Wadsworth, "Counterforce," *The Saturday Review*, July 28, 1962, p. 29.

44 Mandelbaum, p. 191.

45 Alain Enthoven, "1963 Nuclear Strategy Revisited," in Harold P. Ford and Francis X. Winters, S.J., eds., *Ethics and Nuclear Strategy* (Maryknoll, N.Y.: Orbis, 1977), p. 76.

46 Hubert H. Humphrey, "The State of the Question, An Introduction," Center for the Study of Democratic Institutions, *ABM: Yes or No?* (Santa Barbara, CA: Fund for the Republic, 1969), p. 10. McNamara has recently come out with a strong statement in favor of a "no first use" policy. See McGeorge Bundy, George F. Kennan, Robert McNamara and Gerard Smith, "Nuclear Weapons and the Atlantic Alliance."

47 Speech to the Overseas Writers Association Luncheon, International Club, Washington, D.C., January 10, 1974.

48 Harold Brown, *Annual Report, FY 1981*, Washington D.C., p.66.

49 Enthoven, p. 78.

50 Robert C. Aldridge, *The Counterforce Syndrome*, 2nd Edition. Washington D.C.: Institute for Policy Studies, 1979), p. 13.

51 See for example, Jerome Kahan, p. 313.

52 Aldridge, pp. 45-55.

53 Ibid., p. 56-61.

54 Excerpts from the President's speech are printed in the Appendix of Steven E. Miller and Stephen Van Evera, eds., *The Star Wars Controversy* (Princeton: Princeton University Press, 1986), pp. 257-258.

55 Ashton B. Carter, "Directed Energy Missile Defense in Space" (Washington, D.C.: Office of Technology Assessment, 1984). The

full text is printed in *Ibid.* See p. 253.

56 Harold Brown, "The Strategic Defense Initiative," *Survival,*Vol. 27 No. 2 (March/April, 1985), pp 56, 58; and James R. Schlesinger, "Rhetoric and Realities in the Star Wars Debate," *International Security*, Vol. 10, No. 1 (Summer 1985).

57 Miller and Van Evera, eds., p. XV.

58 Alain Enthoven and K. Wayne Smith, *How Much Is Enough?* (New York: Harper and Row, 1971), p. 210.

59 Miller and Van Evera, eds., p. XVI.

60 Schelling, p. 94.

61 John Steinbrunner, "Beyond Rational Deterrence: The Struggle for New Conceptions," *World Politics,* Vol. 28, No. 2 (January, 1976), pp. 223-245.

62 *Ibid.,* p. 226.

63 *Ibid.,* p. 231.

64 In contrast to Steinbrunner, Albert Wohlstetter, "The Delicate Balance of Terror," *Foreign Affairs,* Vol. XXXVII (Jan., 1959) pp. 211-235 is a good example of a scholar who argues that deterrence is hard to maintain and depends on a delicate balance of technological capabilities.

65 Steinbrunner, p. 237.

66 *Ibid.,* p. 243.

67 Thomas Schelling, p. 96.

68 Sidney Lens, *The Day Before Doomsday* (Boston: Beacon, 1977); Robert Gardiner, *The Cool Arm of Destruction* (Philadelphia: Westminster, 1974).

69 Frederick O. Bonkovsky, *International Norms and National Policy* (Grand Rapids, Mich.: Wm. B. Eerdmans, 1980). We will examine Kenneth Waltz's view in Chapter five.

70 John C. Bennett and Harvey Seifert, *U.S. Foreign Policy and Christian Ethics* (Philadelphia: Westminster, 1977); Robert Drinan, "Is Pacifism the Only Option Left for Christians?" in Arthur F. Holmes, ed., *War and Christian Ethics* (Grand Rapids, Mich.: Baker Book House, 1975).

71 Bonkovsky, see Chapter IX, pp. 180-210.

72 Anatol Rapoport, *Strategy and Conscience* (New York: Schocken 1969), p. 25.

73 *Ibid.,* p. 102.

74 Herman Kahn, *On Thermonuclear War* (Princeton: Princeton University Press, 1960), pp. 29-30.

75 G.H. Snyder, Deterrence and Defense: *Toward a Theory of National Security* (Princeton: Princeton University Press, 1961), p. 57.

76   Rapoport, p. 110.
77   Ibid., p. 124.
78   Ibid., p. 125.
79   Ibid., p. 169..
80   Ibid., p. 172.
81   Ibid., p. 188.
82   Ibid., p. 190.
83   Ibid., p. 195.

CHAPTER IV

JUST WAR THEORY AND MODERN WAR

In chapter two we traced just war theory through four stages suggesting that each stage represents a type of political thinking that is present today. Although none of those types of just war theory is fully reproduced today, one can discern the basic outlines of these four types.

The crisis of modern war has produced not only a diversity of approaches to just war theory but also a diversity of conclusions drawn from it.

A good deal of ferment is taking place in the area of just war theory. In the press there have been numerous statements of bishops, archbishops and other church leaders condemning nuclear weapons, often with reference to just war theory. Yet there are several conflicting views of just war theory represented in recent publications. These range from a strong emphasis on the need for counterforce nuclear strategies that depend on double-effect reasoning, to absolute pacifism based on just war theory with an emphasis on non-violent resistance as a replacement for war.[1]

The problem of diversity results, in part, from the fact that war is not a single phenomenon. Warfare ranges from a tribe's defense against cattle thieves to a nation's defense against all-out nuclear attack. This chapter argues that nuclear war cannot be considered a subset of self-defense of the innocent.

All of the actual warfare that is taking place today is non-nuclear. Michael Walzer's book, *Just and Unjust Wars*,[2] is a brilliant demonstration that traditional moral terminology can still make sense in relation to modern, conventional warfare.

In the first section we examine just war theory as a mode of reasoning.

The second section considers the traditional set of just war criteria that was the basis for justifying or condemning any particular war.

The heart of the problem for just war theory is addressed in the third section.   Just war theory contains within it a fundamental tension between teleological and deontological modes of moral evaluation.

In the fourth section we examine the problems that surround the application of the *jus in bello* criterion of discrimination between combatants and non-combatants.   The final section discusses the attempt by three modern just war theorists to relate just war theory to the unique problems of nuclear deterrence.

Just War Theory as a Mode of Reasoning

As a mode of reasoning just war theory has a permanent validity. It tries to find minimally acceptable ways of solving real political problems.   At its best, the just war mode of thought recognizes the acute tension that accompanies attempts at moral responsibility in the face of political conflict.

The just war mode of reasoning seeks to reconcile the need for national defense with the moral imperative of protection for the innocent. It is difficult, or impossible to reconcile the strategic use of large nuclear weapons with protection of the innocent. Some people argue that just war theory necessitates nuclear pacifism.   However, nuclear pacifism directly contradicts certain basic just war assumptions about the inevitability of war and the necessity of defense.

Just Warfare as the Result of Conflicting Duties

Just war theory begins with a presumption against war. According to James Childress, the just war mode of reasoning accepts that there is a *prima facie* duty not to kill anyone under any circumstances. *Prima facie* duties are to be distinguished from both absolute and relative duties.

> If an obligation is viewed as absolute, it cannot be overridden under any circumstances; it has priority over all other obligations with which it might come into

conflict. If it is ruled as relative, the rule stating it is no more than a maxim or rule of thumb that illuminates but does not prescribe what we ought to do. If it is ruled as prima facie, it is intrinsically binding, but it does not necessarily determine one's actual obligation.[3]

The philosopher, William Frankena argues that things such as killing,
... are always prima facie wrong and they are always actually wrong when they are not justified on other moral grounds. They are not in themselves morally indifferent. They may conceivably be justified in certain situations, but they always need to be justified; and even when they are justified there is still one moral point against them.[4]

Just war theorists have traditionally recognized war as a necessary reality because they believe that there are other *prima facie* duties that, under certain circumstances, overrule the duty not to kill. The central conflicting duty is the obligation to protect the innocent and not submit to tyranny. Thus a core assumption of just war theory is that it is sometimes a greater evil to capitulate to injustice than to go to war.

However, even when a *prima facie* duty is overruled and war occurs, the overruled duty should still influence the conduct of war. Thus in war,

... the immediate duty is not to kill or even to injure any particular person but to incapacitate or restrain him. The enemy soldier is not reduced to his role as a combatant, and when he surrenders or is wounded, he ceases to be a combatant because he ceases to be a threat.[5]

This then is the basis for the connection between *jus ad bellum* and *jus in bello* criteria. Behind just war theory is the assumption that human beings have rights which may be abridged by war but never completely eliminated.

The inherent corollary to the assumption that it is sometimes a greater evil to submit to tyranny than to go to war is the converse; it is sometimes better to submit to injustice than to go to war.

The Basis for Moral reasoning about War

Michael Walzer recognized that as prescriptive theory, just war reasoning may often appear ineffectual. Nevertheless moral reasoning is not solely based on results but on the conviction that there is meaning to the moral evaluation of human activity. Walzer suggests that the moral theorist,

> ... must come to grips with the fact that his rules are often violated or ignored—and the deeper realization that, to men of war, the rules often don't seem relevant to the extremity of their situation. But however he does this, he does not surrender his sense of war as a human action, purposive and premeditated for whose effects someone is responsible.[6]

Throughout his book Walzer avoids making any metaphysical claims about the inherent justice or injustice of particular actions or intentions. Inherent good and evil do not lie in the actual activities of soldiers or statesmen. Walzer states that moral judgements about war are fixed only by the opinions of humankind. Nevertheless he indicates that moral reasoning points to a "moral reality of war" that is universally perceived.

> ...there really is a story to tell, a way of talking about wars and battles that the rest of us recognize as morally appropriate. I don't mean that particular decisions are necessarily right or wrong or simply right or wrong, only that there is a way of seeing the world so that moral decision-making makes sense.[7]

Of course Christian just war theorists such as James Childress and J. Bryan Hehir, go a good deal further than this and would argue that the pattern of moral opinion about war is indicative of a moral reality that exists independent of human opinion. This "natural law" of moral reality is grounded in the character of God and the created human order.

It is not surprising that Walzer avoids reference to natural law in light of the morass of difficulties to which natural law thinking is heir. All just war theory, including Walzer's, must have a basis in either natural law, intuition or revelation if it is not to be based simply on human consensus. Walzer's book is full of rights language resistant to rule by the strong or the majority. Walzer does not explain where human rights come from but he concedes a theory of natural law, when he says concerning human rights:

> It is enough to say that they are somehow entailed by our sense of what it means to be a human being. If they are not natural then we have invented them, but natural or invented, they are a palpable feature of our moral world.[8]

The difficulties with natural law theory do not lie in the mode of thinking that postulates a moral structure to human affairs given in the nature of things. The difficulties lie in the attempt to define that order in reference to the particular contingencies of any particular space and time. Walzer avoids that difficulty by emphasizing the validity of a just war mode of reasoning based in human rights without absolutizing the particular criteria of just war theory. To base just war thinking simply on public opinion fatally weakens just war theory.

The Relation between Just War Theory and Pacifism

The just war mode of reasoning has often been defined over against pacifism. The pacifist ideal assumes that killing can never be justified under any circumstances. It is often assumed that the difference between pacifism and just war theory is that pacifism is based on a deontological commitment to the absolute sanctity of life while just war theory assumes a teleological morality in which some killing is allowed. This comparison misses the complexity of both types of reasoning. The pacifist ideal type is certainly partly based on principle. Killing is considered wrong and the pacifist is willing to suffer any consequences rather than kill another person. Pacifists often base their commitment to the non-violent principle on a teleological calculation of the effects of war. Pacifists argue that no matter what the ideals of just war are, once a war gets started, to a large extent moral distinctions become excess baggage and necessity dictates the rules of war.

Just war theory is also a mixed mode of reasoning. It

assumes that a just war provides an exception to the duty not to kill, both on teleological and on deontological grounds. The consequentialist aspect of the ethic assumes that war is inevitable because of human sin. A careful reading of history provides no confidence that "good will" can effect an end to war. Attempts must be made to limit the incidence of war and moderate its effects by moral reason.

The deontological aspect of the theory is the inherent right of opposing unjust aggression. This inherent right holds even if evil consequences result. Walzer suggests that when the strong attack the weak we consider their resistance heroic, even if they are all slaughtered...[9] Paul Ramsey likewise suggests that,

> If non-pacifism is correct it is not first of all because we can foreknow that there can be no greater evil than the consequences supposed to follow from non-resistance to tyranny and aggression but because there is perennial truth to a just war response to the demands of love, whatever the consequences.[10]

Clearly the deontological aspects of both just war and pacifist modes in their extreme forms are opposed to each other. The gap is narrower between the consequentialist aspects of both theories. Pacifists accept the need to limit the incidence of war and moderate its brutality, even if they will not fight. Pacifists who participate in politics must use a just war mode of reasoning in their attempt to influence policy as long as the broader culture will not accept their pacifist assumptions.

Similarly just war theorists can accept the empirical observation that their way is not often effective in limiting war. Insofar as just war principles become less and less possible to maintain in the midst of war, just war theorists may join with pacifists in opposing the outbreak of even "justifiable" wars.

Perhaps the most remarkable development among just war writers is the erosion of the barrier between pacifism and just war theory. Although not all just war theorists would acknowledge that this erosion is valid, some of them are becoming pacifists.

Those who may be called "just war pacifists" retain the basic reasoning structure of just war theory. They do not believe that killing is always absolutely wrong. In theory they believe in the possibility of just wars. In practice they assert that all modern war between nuclear powers runs too great a risk of moving outside the bounds of the just conduct of war. At least war between nuclear powers is considered illegitimate. Some would say that any war runs the risk of escalation to unacceptable levels and must be considered immoral. Writers in the just war tradition who arrive at pacifist conclusions insist that potential consequences of war have modified or terminated a nation's "natural" right to military self-defense. Thus they deny that defense can be held as an unqualified deontological principle.

Just War Theory and the Right of Defense

Of course some just war writers deny that the right of just defense can be abridged. The right wing of just war theory argues that surrender to unjust aggression is even worse than the destruction of the world. Thus Harold O.J. Brown writes:

> A war between the United States and the Soviet Union ... would be terribly destructive and might actually eradicate human civilization or human life itself ... (But) our nation's only hope of remaining free is to be prepared to go to war to defend itself, even at the risk of being destroyed... Perhaps it is the Christians who are the free world's hope of remaining free, for it is we alone who can dare to risk losing much or all in war to forestall what we consider a still greater evil, the world domination of a totalitarian, atheistic system.[11]

Those who elevate the duty to defend "human rights" to the extent that Brown does, essentially make of it an absolute rather than a *prima facie* duty. If a person holds that defense is more important than even human survival, they are no longer within the just war mode of reasoning outlined by Childress. Childress feels the duty to defend against aggression does not have an unqualified deontological force.

Like the duty not to kill, the duty to defend is a *prima facie* duty which may be overruled if the just war criteria are not met.

If the necessity of military resistance to "evil" aggression is considered an absolute duty, then what remains is not a just war theory but only a duty to defend a just cause whatever the cost. The core of the just war theory is not the right of just defense but the moral limitation of defense. In traditional just war theory *jus ad bellum*, (the justification of defense), cannot overrule *jus in bello*, (the just conduct of defense).

Brown's position is essentially ahistorical. Even the strongest and most ruthless tyrannies have seldom lasted more than a hundred years, while nuclear devastation would have permanent effects. Yet some war writers tend to absolutize defense. Even so careful a thinker as John Courtney Murray argued during the cold war that some values were worth blowing up the world to protect.[12] Very few just war writers would defend such a statement today. Murray himself saw just war theory as a median position that avoids both surrender and holocaust. When the question is put in its stark form, most just war writers would have no difficulty choosing surrender over holocaust.

The Definition of the Question

Whether just war reasoning moves in a bellicose or pacifist direction is partially determined by what values are assumed. It is also a function of how the question of just war is defined. Augustine and Aquinas started with the question, "Is it possible for a Christian to participate in war?" That form of the query assumes that war is a questionable activity that needs justification.

Some recent writers begin with a different question. Since they assume a generalized affirmative answer to the ancient question, a subtle shift takes place. Their question becomes in effect, "Given the fact that war is a necessary reality of interstate relations, how can it be brought under the control of reason and morality?" This is the starting position of James

Turner Johnson. As John Courtney Murray and Paul Ramsey put it, "Since nuclear war may be a necessity it must be made a possibility. Its possibility must be created."[13] The form of the question avoids whether or not modern war is morally tolerable. Given technology of modern warfare, the task is either to fit modern warfare into the form of just war theory or to fit just war theory into the form of modern warfare.

In either case, some stretching of just war theory is inevitable. The perimeters of thought about war are set by the necessities of warfare. Not only is just war theory stretched to fit realities for which it was not designed, but the necessities of warfare are shrunk to fit within the expanded criteria of the theory. When this happens, the basic moral assumptions of just war reasoning are violated in the name of realism and the actual political realities of modern war are denied in the name of morality. In order to retain both its integrity and its realism, the just war mode of reasoning must retain its initial anti-war presumption.

The just war mode of reasoning may be summarized in the following propositions. 1. There is a *prima facie* duty not to kill. This duty may be derived from natural law, revelation, intuition or public consensus. It includes the *prima facie* duty not to fight in wars. 2. Governments have a *prima facie* duty to protect their subjects and a *prima facie* right to protect themselves.[14]

Jus ad Bellum Criteria of Justifiable War

There are seven traditional "rules" of *jus ad bellum* that together are held to determine whether or not a war is justifiable. There is some controversy over whether all of these rules must be met to justify a war or only most of them. They are listed in a particular order because the rules are related to each other and each is dependent on the preceding rules.

The first of the *jus ad bellum* rules is 1. legitimate authority. This is the foundational rule because it answers the question, "Who's to judge?" Just war theory cannot operate without a high view of governmental authority. The state is viewed as a moral agent that has a right to make judgements concerning war or peace on behalf of its subjects. If just war theory is applied to revolution some concept of a legitimate authority that represents the people must replace the state as a just authority.

The right to go to war depends on a legitimate authority's assessment of six other points: 2. just cause (defense against aggression[15], 3. just intention (the sincere intention to achieve a just peace), 4. proportionality of the enterprise (the calculation that the probably good effects of going to war will outweigh the evils of the war), 5. last resort (the war is a necessity that cannot be avoided without intolerable loss of legitimate values), 6. reasonable hope of success (the goals of the war can be objectively defined and are reachable) and 7. prior declaration (the rationale for the war has been formally announced and the possibility of further negotiation is not cut off).

The most common objection to these criteria is that they are overly subjective and leave ample room for rationalization and hypocrisy. Only prior declaration can be objectively assessed. Most states that go to war would claim to have met the other six. Nevertheless, the criteria provide a framework for the discussion of the morality of a state's decision to resort to war.

Another objection is that these criteria are full of normative assumptions about the nature of good and evil that cannot be objectively determined. In a pluralistic domestic society, let alone in the international sphere, the criteria cannot arbitrate a decision that would claim wide support. This is a more serious objection if the purpose of the theory is to dampen war by providing a universal moral framework to which all nations could appeal. The criteria were designed for an international society that accepted the unified ideology of Christendom. This is no longer the case. Ronald Reagan, for example, would certainly define a just peace differently than George McGovern or M.S. Gorbachev. Moreover the Church is in no position to mediate the differences.

The criteria do provide a framework of discussion for those

within the Judeo-Christian tradition, even without their former power as a universal framework of appeal. Some would say they served that function admirably for Americans during the Vietnam War.[16]

The most significant problem with the categories is that they were formulated in the Middle Ages when warfare had a different meaning. The categories were designed for war between princes and their warriors in which a trial by arms was thought to provide a practical and possibly just way, (given the sovereignty of God), to settle a dispute. War between nuclear powers is no longer a contest of strength but a bargaining process that raises different moral questions. In particular, the traditionalist criteria do not address the unique problems of deterrence. They give no guidance as to how to evaluate the moral significance of different levels of threat and of risk.

What, for example, is a justifiable cause for going to war when both sides have the ability to devastate each other and a good part of the world in minutes? Just war criteria clearly rule out a world destroying nuclear war. But they cannot adjucate between different strategies of risk intended to prevent such a disaster.

Can an "intention to achieve a just peace" justify a war between superpowers that risks permanent damage to the planet? How can proportionality between good and evil effects be rationally considered when the prospective damage of a nuclear war requires that the conflict be considered a war between absolute good and evil? The ends of a war inevitably inflate to match the means considered necessary. What is the meaning of last resort when any resort risks not only the destruction of a government but the annihilation of a substantial part of a society? How can the word "success" remain meaningful apart from the total avoidance of war in the first place? Can the chance of success below the level of nuclear weapons be termed reasonable when even a small risk exists that war would bring global holocaust?

The just war mode of reasoning is a necessary means of considering the morality of nuclear war. The duty of a state to protect its people must be considered in relation to the duty not to kill. However, the *jus ad bellum* categories do not provide meaningful criteria by which the dangers of nuclear war can be assessed. Instead they further the illusion that modern war between superpowers is similar to war in the 17th century, only a little more destructive.

Nuclear weapons require that the just war concern for an adequate response to unjust aggression be supplemented by an even greater concern for the prevention of nuclear war. The meaning of defense and security must be rethought in light of the new nature of war and the risks involved in all conflict that involves superpowers.

The Tension between *Jus ad Bellum* and *Jus in Bello* in Just War Theory

The Problem of Contradiction between *Jus ad Bellum* and *Jus in Bello*

Michael Walzer points out that, "the dualism of *jus ad bellum* and *jus in bello* is at the heart of all that is most problematic in the moral reality of war."[17] Just war theory assumes that war is always a crime. A justifiable war in which both sides are right is not conceivable in just war terms. Both sides may be wrong and both may have some elements of right on their sides, but ultimately war represents the breakdown of moral restraints and the immoral attempt to gain or prevent advantage by killing. At least one side must be labeled the aggressor if just war theory is to be applicable.

This is a teleological mode of reasoning with a deontological limitation. The problem lies in the fact that these two aspects of the argument may come into conflict. The limits that *jus in bello* place on the conduct of war are discrimination and proportionality. Proportionality is a teleological limit that says nothing should be done that creates more evil than the good it achieves. Calculation of such things in war is difficult but the rule is inherently logical. Even in the moral chaos of war it preserves the meaning of *jus ad bellum* because it requires that a greater evil only be stopped by a lesser evil. The justifiability of war is based on the logic of proportionality.

The *jus in bello* limit of discrimination between combatants and noncombatants is less clear in its connection to *jus ad bellum*. If a lesser evil such as killing can be used to prevent a greater evil, and if the intentional killing of non-combatants is held to be a lesser evil than losing the war, then why not kill non-combatants, as long as it is necessary and considered proportionate?

The tension between *jus ad bellum* and *jus in bello* is inherent in just war theory with or without nuclear weapons. Nuclear bombs simply bring that tension into sharper relief. It is the ultimate tension between teleological and deontological modes of thought. Just war theory attempts to utilize both modes of reasoning. Either mode, when pushed to the extreme, excludes the other. *Jus ad bellum* is a teleological argument which, when pressed by necessity, excludes the deontological principle that, by its own logic, cannot give in to the necessity that presses on consequentialist reasoning.

Utilitarian and absolutist modes of thought can only co-exist when the stakes are relatively low, when the absolutist rules are enforceable, or when, for whatever reason, both sides keep the rules. When the pressures of necessity rise, deontological and teleological modes of thought come into conflict and one or the other must be chosen. The new factor in modern war is that the extreme pressure of necessity not only characterizes the "darkest hour" that once marked the climax of a war. It has also intruded into the everyday life called "peace."

Nuclear weapons, and to a lesser extent the whole web of modern technological warfare have made defense impossible within the boundaries of *jus in bello* limitations. The basic problem is that victory in warfare cannot be obtained by a country that does not break the traditional rules of just warfare. In just war theory it must at least be possible for a "just" party that adheres to the *jus in bello* rules to gain victory over an aggressor who does not. Just war theory cannot hold together if its rules guarantee defeat for those who hold them. If victory cannot be attained within the bounds of *jus in bello* behavior then no "just" party can go to war with a "reasonable chance of success." Therefore no nation could meet the requirements of *jus ad bellum*, including reasonable chance of success, if it intended to keep within *jus in bello*, unless victory was possible within the bounds of *jus in bello*.

This has always been a problem for just war theory. It is a major reason why *jus in bello* rules are so often ignored in war. If a country is convinced of the justice of its cause and moral restraints appear to threaten its chance for success, there is a great pressure to relax or abandon the moral restraints. Thus Clausewitz wrote, "...the ruthless user of force who shrinks from no amount of bloodshed must gain an advantage if his opponent does not do the same."[18]

Just war theory depends on the assumption that while just conduct of a war may concede an advantage to unjust aggressors, it does not ensure their victory. Otherwise just war becomes politically impossible. Many observers and military leaders have concluded that warfare with moral rules is indeed politically impossible. If *jus ad bellum* is held strongly enough it necessitates the abandonment of *jus in bello*. It was this form of thinking that certainly led the upright British to obliteration bombing when it appeared that Germany was winning the war.

While the problem was significant in the pre-nuclear world, it was not decisive. The advantage given up by fighting justly against an unjust opponent could be overcome. Nuclear weapons have erased that possibility. Military strategists generally assume that an enemy that is willing to use nuclear weapons cannot be defeated or withstood by a country that will not. Unless a nation is shielded by nuclear threats of an ally, it cannot wage war against an opponent that is willing and able to use nuclear weapons.

The Traditional Solution to the Tension

The traditional just war solution is to assert even more strongly that both sides must keep to the *jus in bello* rules. If both sides keep the rules no one is put at a disadvantage and both sides are better off than if neither observed moral limits. This is hypothetically a good solution and may even have enjoyed some moderate success when Christendom or European cosmopolitanism ensured a common agreement as to what the *jus in bello* rules entailed. However the dubious history of twentieth century warfare gives little hope that such a happy solution is a practical possibility.

If, in practice, one side does not keep the rules of *jus in bello*, a just party is still required to keep them, according to traditional theory, even if such a policy leads to defeat. Thus *jus in bello* is elevated over *jus ad bellum*. This was the characteristic stance of the fourth stage of "secularized" just war theory. In light of the wars of religion and the routine protestations of justice by all parties in a dispute, *jus ad bellum* considerations were devalued in the rules of just war. Not that they were considered unimportant in theory, but in practice they were not an effective restraint on war. *Jus in bello* rules appeared to at least have a chance of reducing war's brutality if not undermined by an overemphasis on the justice of the cause.

Such is the basic position of Paul Ramsey. Ramsey assumes a rigorous *jus ad bellum* that is based, not primarily on justice, but on love. The bulk of Ramsey's writing is not on *jus ad bellum* but on the necessity of finding realistic ways to stay within *jus in bello* rules. While Ramsey is known for his ingenuity in stretching the *jus in bello* rules through intricate reasoning, he does not allow them to be set aside under pressure of necessity. Nor does he admit that fighting justly must result in defeat.

In his first book on war, Ramsey attempts to protect both *jus ad bellum* and *jus in bello* by calling for the courage to defy nuclear blackmail and neither threaten to use large nuclear bombs nor bow to those who do. He says,

> It is right that the enemy be made to realize that he will have to exceed the limits or warfare to gain his ends, that he will have to destroy utterly where he thought to conquer and to bend.[19]

Ramsey later found a way to justify deterrence with large nuclear weapons, but at this point his argument retains the deontological element in just war theory by preferring national destruction to what he considers the immoral options of surrender or indiscriminate warfare. Surrender would represent the end of *jus ad bellum* while indiscriminate war would spell the end of *jus in bello*. The way to avoid both these dangers, according to Ramsey is to refuse to make policy decisions on the basis of consequences alone. Ramsey says the destruction of humankind is not the only and greatest evil. In any case, Ramsey points out that to deny nuclear blackmail is not to choose national destruction over surrender or immoral warfare but is to choose the risk of national destruction over the other two options.[20]

Ramsey's early proposal is a heroic one and may provide the best theoretical way to preserve just war theory in the face of nuclear weapons: don't use them and don't submit to them. One wonders how many nuclear warheads would have to fall on the U.S. before the heroics were abandoned. I suspect that very few cities or even counterforce targets would need to be hit to produce an intolerable pressure on policy makers to either surrender or retaliate with nuclear weapons.

Ramsey suggests that the principle problem of just war theory is not the determination of just limits. The problem is,

> ... where are the men in whose minds and where is the community of men in whose very ethos the propelling reason for ever engaging in war also itself lays down intrinsic moral limits upon how the defense of civilized life should proceed?[21]

Perhaps Ramsey realized that a community with a vigorous just war ethos did not exist and this led him to change to a justification of nuclear deterrence.

"Supreme Emergency" as a Solution to the Tension

Michael Walzer suggests that the problem may be mitigated by a concept of "supreme emergency." In essence his idea is that discrimination must be fully maintained by a just party unless a supreme emergency arises. Walzer's definition of supreme emergency is very narrow. A supreme emergency cannot be called for the purpose of shortening the war or even preventing defeat, unless defeat means the annihilation of the state and the enthronement of tyranny. If there is imminent danger of the utter destruction of a society's most cherished values it is unrealistic to expect it to adhere to *jus in bello*.

In the supreme emergency, the principle of discrimination is not abolished. But a society may be forced to break its rules anyway. Thus necessity may force the following reflection: "I dare to say that our history will be nullified and our future condemned unless I accept the burdens of criminality here and now."[22] Even in the supreme emergency it is a criminal act to kill the innocent which is always "a kind of blasphemy against our deepest moral commitments." In the final analysis, necessity does come into play.

> These, then are the limits of the realm of necessity. Utilitarian calculation can force us to violate the rules of war only when we are face to face not merely with defeat, but with a defeat likely to bring disaster to a political community. But those calculations have no similar effects when what is at stake is only the speed or the scope of the victory.[23]

On the basis of this reasoning, Walzer is able both to justify the initial Allied decision to undertake obliteration bombing and to condemn the atom bombing of Japan.

Walzer argues his position very convincingly. Without denying the irreducible element of tension between *jus ad bellum* and *jus in bello*, his proposal retains *jus in bello* as an important and usually inviolable part of the conduct of war without giving up the ultimate supremacy of *jus ad bellum* and the possibility of defense.

There are three weaknesses to his argument. The first is elasticity in the concept of supreme emergency. Supreme emergency is the principle that proportionality has ultimate precedence over discrimination. The conditions that define a supreme emergency are prey to extreme subjectivity during the chaos of war.

Secondly, there is no inherent reason why the proportionality argument that governs emergency should not be extended. If *jus in bello* can be abridged in the event of a supreme emergency, why not also to prevent a supreme emergency from occurring? The same argument Walzer uses to justify preventive war for a just cause could be used to suppress *jus in bello* before a supreme emergency occurs. If one waits for the supreme emergency before breaking the rules of war it may, by then, be too late.

The third and most telling argument is that nuclear weapons have rendered all warfare involving superpowers a supreme emergency. With nuclear weapons, not only war, but peace as well, meets Walzer's definition of supreme emergency. The danger that threatens is arguably greater than any in the history of the world and it is always an imminent danger.

Holding the Tension in Relative Balance

Another attempt to cut the gordian knot has been made by James T. Johnson. For Johnson, a major criteria for an adequate system of moral guidance is how well it bridges the gap between the ideal and the real. "That is, does it produce practical moral guidance as well as identify the relevant moral values for the situation at hand."[24] In light of his emphasis on the utility of moral guidance, Johnson poses a challenge to those who morally reject all use of nuclear weapons: the burden is on them to find morally acceptable military ways to combat evil in the world.[25]

Johnson defines his task in terms of three questions: How can we use our current arsenal of nuclear weapons in ways that do the least damage to the principles of proportionality and discrimination?; How can we maintain deterrence?; and How can we develop a defensive system that will make it more possible to defend ourselves within the *jus in bello* rules?[26]

Johnson's analysis of current nuclear weapons and strategy is realistic and bleak. He concludes that "only at the limits of reason, if there" could either strategic or tactical/theatre nuclear warfare be considered just. He says

> "...there exist significant moral reasons against even
> lowest levels of such countercombatant use, reasons that
> gain strength the farther up the escalation ladder one
> proceeds. Current strategic nuclear weapons are simply too
> grossly destructive to be employed with restraint in
> nearly any conceivable military situation, and their use
> even against a legitimate (that is, a combatant) target
> would entail such foreseeable collateral harm to
> non-combatants as to cast grave doubts on the morality of
> such use."[27]

Nevertheless, Johnson sees little point in denouncing
nuclear weapons and proposes a kind of hierarchy of negative
preferability.

The less destructive, the more accurate and hence the more
discriminating the weapon, the better. He points out that
conventional weapons can also be extremely destructive and
suggests that armaments should not be judged on the basis of
whether or not they are nuclear but on their intended use.[28]
The only legitimate use he foresees is in limited, counterforce
warfare. Even in such discriminating use, he points out that
the long-term effects of radiation would be indiscriminate.

Even in light of his bleak analysis of the justifiability of
any nuclear warfare, Johnson's judgements are strictly relative.
He repeatedly argues that counterforce use of nuclear weapons
is much closer to the just war tradition than counter-value use
and mildly concludes that the use of heavy megatonage
thermonuclear weapons, "should be avoided wherever
possible and restrained if avoidance is impossible..."[29]

Johnson's lack of any strong denunciation of nuclear warfare
(let alone deterrence) is based on three fundamental
assumptions. The first is that nuclear weapons technology is in
itself neutral. The moral task is not to judge technology, but
human intentions. He says,

> "... it is not the weapons of war in our time but the
> assumptions about war that are morally questionable.
> Weapons are but tools of human intentions, and the reason
> we now live in a world where entire populations are
> threatened by nuclear missiles is that we have come to

regard such threats as appropriate."[30]

As I have argued above, I believe that such an assumption is naive. Technologies are almost never neutral. For better and for worse, our inventions shape our social existence, often in ways that lie beyond our intentions. Seldom is a technology all good or all evil. Even nuclear weapons contain moral ambiguity. But the weapons themselves embody an overwhelming evil by the threat posed by their physical existence.

Johnson's second assumption is that the only responsible moral task is to work with the present reality of nuclear defense policy and try to bring it closer to the principles of just war tradition. He says,

> "To argue against the strategic nuclear arsenal without making clear what alternative should replace it amounts to either a mistaken logic or a denial that any values this culture has are worth preserving by war."[31]

Such linear logic poses a legitimate challenge to nuclear critics but is also misleading. Taken by itself it would silence most of the social protest in history. The unspoken presumption is that legitimate alternatives must be politically realistic to the political, economic and social regime of our time. On this advice, slavery would still be with us.

Moral perception often outstrips the technical expertise or social upheaval necessary to create an alternative. Johnson's realism is a recipe for the preservation of the *status quo*. Sometimes all the politically realistic alternatives that can be visualized are completely unacceptable. The very best of Johnson's negative strategic preferences (restrained, morally intentioned, counterforce strikes), are nightmare visions of literally incalculable horror. To judge them a lesser evil is certainly formally correct but obscures the enormity of evil they represent. It can even lead apparently intelligent strategists to speak of "winning" a nuclear war. The rhetoric of counterforce limited nuclear warfare has become the most potent means for legitimizing the possibility of nuclear warfare.

These arguments do not silence Johnson's challenge to nuclear critics to find alternatives to the nuclear arsenal. His proposals to strengthen U.S. conventional forces are helpful directions to explore. More radical critics must also struggle with how to preserve the values they love.

Johnson's third assumption directly addresses the problem of how to resolve the tension between *jus ad bellum* and *jus in bello*. The burden of his book is that a tension must be preserved between the two and just means must be created that are suitable to the ends of justifiable war. However, the tenor of his book supports his conclusion that "...when one is sure of one's own justice and of the enemy's injustice, one may temporarily and in specific cases go beyond the limits, even harming non-combatants."[32]

Johnson emphasizes that this is only permissible if there are no other options available. Citing Franciscus de Victoria for support, Johnson suggests that the whole sweep of the just war tradition, at least up to the last century, puts *jus ad bellum* first and subordinates proportion and discrimination to the rightness of the cause of war.[33]

Prior to the invention of gunpowder and the application of the double effect principle to the use of cannons, it would be difficult to show how early writers relativized *jus in bello*. Even with Victoria, the amount of indiscriminate destruction envisaged is very limited. Johnson's implicit, relative justification of our current strategic arsenal (until a more proportionate *jus ad bellum* above *jus in bello* not just in specific cases but as an ongoing reality of strategic deterrence. By doing so, he adopts the same policy of "supreme emergency" which we have seen in Michael Walzer. Unlike Walzer, he disguises his ultimate withdrawal from the just war tradition by advocating a counterforce strategy which is relatively more just than counterpopulation warfare.

If just war theory is to retain its basic structure of a teleological argument, founded in love (Augustine) and with deontological limits to what can be done in war, then Johnson's relative critique of U.S. defense policy has moved outside the perimeters of the tradition.

Nuclear weapons have created an insolvable problem for just war theory. The tension that has always existed between *jus ad bellum* and *jus in bello* has reached the point of contradiction in the case of war between nuclear powers.

The Problem of Discrimination in Modern War

Proportionate reason might be willing to sacrifice the principle of discrimination in order to retain the possibility of just defense in modern war. But discrimination is fundamental to just war theory. *Jus ad bellum* is based, not only on the prevention of aggression, but also on the preservation of human rights. Even if the proportionate killing of non-combatants prevents aggression, it inherently undermines the *jus ad bellum* purpose of preserving the rights of the innocent.

Discrimination is essential to just war theory because war can only be justified if it preserves the innocent from aggression. The justification for a war is severely undermined if it becomes a wholesale attack on the innocent. The innocent must be protected in war so that the human rights basis of *jus ad bellum* is not undermined. Roman Catholic authors commonly ascribe a natural law force to the protection of the innocent in war. Killing of the innocent, when directly intended, is not just *prima facie* wrong, it is absolutely wrong.

Discrimination faces more than just the problem of application in modern warfare. It also faces internal problems of definition and consistency in relation to mass warfare. The fundamental problem is the ascription of guilt and innocence. Guilt and innocence are moral and legal terms that assume a degree of individual responsibility on the part of those who are so judged. In warfare it is impossible to either find an impartial judge or render a verdict on every enemy to be killed. The just war solution is to apply a rough rule of thumb that ascribes guilt or non-innocence to a general class of people that is objectively involved in furthering the unjust aggression of the enemy. This group of "combatants" ranges from the obvious soldier with his rifle to more ambiguous classes of people such as civilians who produce plastic seat covers for jeeps. As John C. Ford, S.J., ably pointed out, the existence of grey areas between combatants and non-combatants does not in itself invalidate the distinction.[34] Ford argued that in 1944 even the most liberal definitions of combatants would not cover more than 25% of the civilian population of major cities.

The diffusion of militarily useful professions throughout society has increased dramatically since the end of World War II. The grey areas are significantly larger in American society today than they were when Ford wrote his influential article. The definitional problems with the term "combatant" are also increasing. Yet it is still true that a substantial majority of civilian society could not be labeled combatants.

The problem with discrimination is the equation of innocence with non-combatant status and the equation of guilt with combatancy.

A combatant may be killed on the basis of membership in a group that is considered a threat even though he or she may be individually "innocent." In warfare, combatants must be killed without differentiating between voluntary recruits who may be trained, patriotic killers and unwilling draftees who will never, in fact, fire their guns. Combatant "guilt" is a necessarily arbitrary designation based on membership in a class of people which corporately appears to threaten the opponents' security.

Just war theorists may deny that guilt is ascribed to any individual combatant. It is the action of the whole group that is condemned. Individual combatants are killed by necessity as the only means of stopping the corporate aggression. This is a helpful distinction but it does not solve the problem of the rights of the innocent. Innocent combatants are killed in wars. The problem would be much less severe if all combatants freely chose to fight in the war. Unfortunately that has seldom been the case in the history of warfare.[35]

The designation of guilt, or non-innocence, is not necessarily related to the personal responsibility of the individual combatant. The combatant may hate war and personally wish to have nothing to do with it. He may be like the reputed majority of U.S. soldiers who never fire their rifles, even when ordered to in combat. Nevertheless as part of a threatening group, combatants may be killed because they are combatants, not because they have done or even intended to do anything wrong.

Modern warfare has exacerbated this problem through the practice of long-distance killing. In more "primitive" forms of war a soldier was usually killed in the act of personal combat. While the soldier might have been from an oppressed class and forced to fight, he was at least involved in objectively aggressive behavior. While he may have been subjectively innocent he was objectively guilty. In modern warfare a soldier who is killed by a bomb may be subjectively and objectively innocent.

The converse difficulty exists concerning the innocence of non- combatants. The non-combatant's innocence is an innocence by association. Even if the non-combatant is a war-monger who incites hatred of the enemy and urges every eligible person to enlist in the marines, he or she is still "innocent" and may not be killed according to *jus in bello* rules. Of course large numbers of non-combatants are indeed innocent of the issues over which a war is fought. Children are an obvious example. Discrimination protects many innocent people. But association with combatant or non-combatant groups does not by itself establish the guilt or innocence of individuals.

Many combatants would be non-combatants if they could. And many non-combatants sustain a war-effort. The principle of discrimination is a valuable, practical means of preserving the lives of many innocent people. Nevertheless modern war inevitably attacks the rights of the innocent by the relatively arbitrary adjudication of who is innocent.

Some just war advocates concede this point and argue on the basis of proportionate reason that discrimination at least protects some innocent people and preserves the ideal that the innocent should not be intentionally attacked. Discrimination may not fully guard the rights of the innocent but it is certainly better than nothing. This is the direction of argument that Michael Walzer took when he wrote in 1967:

For the bar against the systematic slaughter of civilians is of such immense benefit to mankind that it could only be broken by a country absolutely certain not only that the immediate gains would be enormous, but that the shattered limit would never again be of any use.[36]

This form of argument for discrimination is utilitarian and teleological. A significant shift has taken place from a view of discrimination as an inviolable deontological principle to a teleological principle that fits under the rubric of proportionality. If discrimination is considered an aspect of proportionality and not an inviolable independent principle, then the tension between *jus ad bellum* and *jus in bello* is overcome. It is overcome, however, at a price most just war theorists might think too steep. In the heat of war, or in the face of nuclear threats, discrimination as an aspect of proportionality may be rationalized far more easily than if it is considered an absolute duty.

The principle of discrimination between combatants and non-combatants may lose its deontological force without undermining the absolute principle that the innocent should not be intentionally attacked. If combatants may be judged guilty by association and destroyed by necessity, even though they may not all be individually guilty, then a similar argument could be logically applied to attacking non-combatants in a modern war. It is non-combatants who pay for a war, provide the material and political support necessary for its continuance, and have the greatest ability to bring a war to an end through political pressure.

Even though non-combatants may include many innocent people, the idea of guilt by association or corporate guilt, combined with the military utility of attacking them could be used to justify such as attack. If it is true that whole societies war against each other in modern war, rather than just military elites, then there is no inherent reason for defending the non-military segments of society from the effects of the war if necessity indicates otherwise.

When the principle of discrimination was developed, the connections between combatancy and guilt and between non-combatancy and innocence were much stronger.

Discrimination began with a concern for the clearly innocent. Beginning with Augustine's argument that priests and religious orders should never be attacked, ever longer lists of professions were specified. By the time of Christine de Pisan in the fifteenth century there were elaborate lists of those professions which were considered non-combatant, complete with the reasoning that went into each selection. War was a class affair fought by soldiers who chose or inherited their profession. Just war theory excluded non-professionals from the conflict.[37] The actual conduct of war was never that precise, but the ideal was clear.

Discrimination no longer primarily distinguishes between guilty and innocent individuals. In modern war the question is where a country may direct its missiles and bombs. The just war principle that the innocent should not be attacked still retains its force as a deontological principle. But it cannot be kept under the conditions of modern war. Non-combatant immunity is an important second best. It is no longer an absolute principle that protects the rights of the innocent, but a proportionate rule that lessens the destructiveness of modern war. Modern warfare necessarily attacks human rights.

Just War Theory and Deterrence: the Morality of Intention

The basic, primary utility of nuclear weapons lies not in their detonation in actual conflict but in their use as a threat to maintain deterrence. Deterrence is the central strategy of modern warfare. Yet deterrence does not neatly fit under *jus ad bellum* or *jus in bello*. Deterrence precedes and circumscribes the boundaries of actual warfare. It underlies all other military strategies. While deterrence has much to do with preventing war, it has little to do with its condemnation or justification.

Deterrence is an embarrassment and a puzzle to just war theory. In terms of *jus ad bellum*, deterrence appears to be the only possible means of resisting unjust aggression. Thus deterrence is needed to uphold the basic premise of just war theory. Deterrence appears to rest on the intent to do something that would massively violate every principle of *jus in bello*. Deterrence provides a final revelation of incompatibility of *jus ad bellum* and *jus in bello*.

Just War Deterrence on the Basis of Counterforce Policy

There have been three significant attempts to justify deterrence in the context of just war theory. The first important attempt was Paul Ramsey's. The problem for Ramsey is that strategic nuclear weapons cannot be deterred with fractional kiloton tactical weapons. Massive strategic weapons that can rip away a portion of a country must be deterred by similar monstrosities. City strikes are deterred with city strikes. That appears to spell the end of just war theory. Classical moral theology always held that an intention to do evil is wrong. In 1961, Ramsey argued vigorously against strategic nuclear deterrence. Basic to the advocacy in his first book, of limited unilateral disarmament, was the belief that if it was wrong to use large nuclear weapons, it must also be wrong to threaten to use them. Ramsey puts the issue starkly by drawing an analogy to domestic society. He suggests that it is wrong to get at another person's murderous intent by threatening his children. Thus Ramsey ruled out the deterrent possession of weapons that could not be actually used. He also argued from Herman Kahn that a deterrent was not credible if there was no real intent to follow through.[38]

Two years later (1963) Ramsey changed his mind and worked out a highly subtle moral justification for retaining large nuclear weapons for deterrent purposes. A significant factor in this change was his reversal on the necessity of intent to back up deterrence. Ramsey came to believe the position he had earlier ridiculed, that the simple existence of large nuclear weapons was sufficient to deter the Russians. Intent to use them was not necessary.

Nevertheless, Ramsey believed that there must be some valid, moral use for strategic weapons or their possession could not be justified. The valid use he proposed is a counterforce use against hardened missile silos, etc.. The U.S. should not intend to use large nuclear weapons against cities but through the possession of large weapons for counterforce purposes the U.S. can deter the Russians. Deterrence would be accomplished because, 1. counterforce warfare at its highest will involve great civilian "collateral damage" and can serve as a deterrent without murderous intent, because of the principle of double-effect. 2. Great weapons have two inherent possible uses. Although we may say we will only use them on military targets, the enemy can never know we will not use them on cities. 3. If the above two reasons are not sufficient, "then an apparent resolution to fight war irrationally or at best an ambiguity about our intentions may have to be our expressed policy."[39]

Ramsey's first point bases deterrence on a willingness to use nuclear weapons in a counterforce way which will inevitable be disproportionate. His second and third points depend on the appearance of an intent to use them on cities if necessary. Ramsey's basis for deterrence assumes that the willingness to act with intentional disproportion is morally permissible as long as discrimination is retained as a secret intention.

Ramsey attempts to get past this apparent separation of discrimination from its base in proportionality by arguing that the potential for disproportionate use implied in the deterrent threat is not itself disproportionate to the political good of deterrence. The question that must be asked of this tortuous logic is: can intentional, potential disproportion be compared to its hoped for deterrent effect in such a way as to produce a result that is intelligible? This writer does not believe that is possible. Intended, disproportionate use is still a means of threatening "the other man's children in order to get at his murderous intent."

Ramsey's resolution of the problem of proportionality can work only if the facts to be compared are carefully selected. If you compare the destructiveness of a major counterforce attack with the good of restraining Russia, it is difficult to maintain that proportionality is met. If you compare the intent to wreak the damage of a counterforce strike with the good of restraining Soviet aggression, the traditional mode of reasoning is still violated. If you compare the good of world peace and the maintenance of the deterrence with the danger that the intent to wreak the damage of a counterforce strike might have to be carried out, then proportionality may be met.

Of course the assumption must be that the danger will not usher in the actuality of nuclear war. Even with the loaded deck of Ramsey's proportionality equation, the proportionality is dependent upon the prediction that the counterforce strike will remain no more than a danger. Only as long as it works is it possible to argue that deterrence maintains more good than it produces evil.

In Ramsey's equation he has only compared the best possible outcome of deterrence (world peace), with the worst possible outcome of the removal of the deterrence (universal tyranny or the unrestrained use of nuclear weapons by one side). A more accurate comparison would be between the dangers of deterrence and the dangers of nuclear disarmament. Unfortunately neither set of dangers can be measured in any meaningful way.

Ramsey's use of proportionality is also inadequate in assessing the actual good and evil of deterrence. Ramsey compares the best possible good of deterrence (world peace), with a very limited assessment of the evil of deterrence (that it is expensive and creates the possibility of our initiating a counterforce nuclear strike). An assessment of the present actual, as well as the future possible, costs of deterrence is beyond the scope of this chapter. However a limited discussion of these costs will be taken up in Chapter Six.

Ramsey obviously does not want nuclear war. He recognizes that most arguments would become irrelevant once there was an exchange of large nuclear weapons. Ramsey's position is therefore based on the necessity he perceives of being able to fight a limited nuclear war with small nuclear weapons while at the same time limiting through deterrence the temptation of either side to escalate towards megaton bombs.

Ramsey's attempt to argue from just war principles to deterrence is a failure.[40] But the problem he perceived and tried to address remains unsolved. J. Bryan Hehir comments, "The point is not that any moralist finds the paradox of deterrence acceptable; it is rather the paucity of alternatives which are both morally acceptable and politically viable."[41]

The problem is that the real intent of the threat is to prevent what is threatened! The weakness of the argument is that no one can guarantee that the deterrence will never fail. If it fails, the deterrent threat, no matter how pacifistic its fundamental motivation, could become the stimulus to genocide.

Just War Deterrence on the Basis of Disguised Intent

A second major attempt to retain deterrence in a context of just war theory is made by J. Bryan Hehir. Unlike Ramsey, Hehir does not believe that any use of nuclear weapons in warfare can be morally justified. Hehir argues that the purpose of nuclear weapons is deterrence and nothing else. They are not made to be used and the intent to use them is not necessary to maintain the deterrent. There is a clear difference, according to Hehir, between deterrence policy and strategic policy. Deterrence policy has to do with declared intention and psychological warfare, while strategic policy has to do with actual intentions and plans. Hehir says,

> The direct transition from intention to action ignores the institutional structure of the levels of strategic policy which allow ample room to distinguish declared intention from planned action.[42]

In other words, stated national policy is not necessarily related to actual intentions at the bureaucratic level. According to Hehir, the goal of deterrence policy is to prevent war. He says,

> If conflict occurs this policy has failed and we move into a new realm of action, combat policy...the weapons exist to be not used; their purpose is to threaten, not to strike. If it is granted that this is the primary and actual purpose of these weapons, then the objection that they are indiscriminate weapons which can neither be used nor intended to be used is not pertinent. It does not pertain to their designed function; it would only be pertinent if the weapons designed for deterrence were perverted from their

intended use and moved into the order of action termed combat policy.[43]

Hehir has succeeded in proposing a solution that is both realistically perceptive of the way in which governments work, and which bypasses the major just war objections to nuclear deterrence. He breaks the logical link between declared future policy and real future policy. The goals of declared policy and real policy are ultimately the same. Declared future policy has the goal of preventing war right now by giving the appearance of being willing to commit and if necessary suffer a holocaust. Real future policy that would become operational in case of war also has the primary goal of avoiding the holocaust. The two kinds of policy are only apparently contradictory. They both aim to prevent nuclear holocaust. The intention of a deterrent threat is not aggressive but pacifistic.

This unity of intention is held to justify the deception. It also provides the basis for avoiding the just war objection that the deterrent threat is disproportionate and indiscriminate. The very purpose of the threat is to prevent indiscriminate and disproportionate warfare.

Hehir's solution is only a partial one in regard to just war criteria. No matter what the intent of the threat is, the actual threat remains disproportionate and indiscriminate. To repeat Ramsey's phrase, it is still a way of getting at the enemy's criminal intent by threatening his children. According to traditional moral theology, it makes little difference that there is no intent to carry out the threat. The threat is still immoral. The fact that everyone knows that it might be a bluff because declared and actual policy are seldom the same, does not help much. The value of the threat lies only in the degree to which it is believed.

Hehir's solution raises additional moral problems that are unrelated to just war theory. Presumably only the President should know the actual intended use of the weapons. Thus the moral problem remains for all the rest of the people who can only know the external threat. Hehir's theory sounds like the midnight musing of a commander-in-chief. By definition it cannot provide the basis for a policy debate.

Intent is a subjective category. No action or policy can be judged solely on the basis of an intended result irrespective of planned preparations. Can a president even know what his own intent will be or how he will respond at the beginning of World War III? To judge a threat moral because of a secret intent not to carry it out assumes that action can be simply the result of internal moral decision that is independent of the structural pressures that deeply influence difficult decisions.

If the real intent of a president is subject to change under stress, the same especially holds true for a whole government. In a period of crisis, Ronald Reagan may not intend to use nuclear weapons while George Schultz may intend to use them. With division inside a cabinet the pressure against a secret pacifist intent contrary to stated policy would be immense.

Deterrence depends upon the credibility of a threat. Deterrence is a psychological reality that is undermined by a secret nuclear pacifist intent. More likely, the pacifist intent is undermined by external action to back up the threat. There is a closer tie between external action (the threat and the war preparations necessary to make it credible), and internal disposition (the secret intent), than Hehir admits. What people do affects what they think, especially if they do it for years on end. The same burden does not fall on an ethicist who can devise a neat barrier between intention and action without having to bear the weight of massive preparations for the unintended nuclear war.

Unless the intent *not* to use nuclear weapons was programmed into the technocracy that controls the weapons there would always be the chance of their use by a preprogrammed bureaucracy. If the nuclear pacifist intent was programmed into the bureaucratic structure, the danger of a leak would make deterrence very unstable.

Deterrence is not static. It is a changing structure that is continually affected by complex decision-making and bargaining. Hehir's escape hatch from the nuclear quagmire assumes that the non- use of nuclear weapons can be the result of a simple rational decision at the last minute. The type of bargaining that took place in the Cuban Missile crisis illustrates the way in which a crisis can be entered incrementally and just as gradually get out of control.

The idea that a President might be a secret nuclear pacifist is a reassuring thought but it does not solve the moral problem of deterrence. Nor could a President escape responsibility if a nuclear war should occur, by appealing to his intentions. You cannot tie someone to the railroad tracks and then escape responsibility after they're hit by saying that you intended to cut them loose in time!

Hehir accepts the reasoning that the simplest and most stable possible deterrent is provided by mutually assured destruction (M.A.D.). Hehir accepts M.A.D. not because he likes it or thinks it a permanent solution to the nuclear dilemma, but because he sees no other politically viable solution within the boundaries of just war theory. In contrast, Ramsey, like James Johnson rejects M.A.D. as intolerably immoral because it threatens non-combatant populations. Ramsey argues for a counterforce policy that refuses to target civilian populations.

Just war theory cannot provide any adequate means of judging between M.A.D. and counterforce modes of deterrence. Neither approach can be justified under *jus in bello*. Ramsey and Johnson argue that counterforce provides at least a relative kind of discrimination and the attempt to limit war. But it can equally be argued that M.A.D. is closer in intent to the avoidance of any indiscriminate warfare. Both approaches contain ethical assumptions combined with differences in perception or prediction. Either position may be considered an extension of the just war mode of thinking. But neither can be justified under traditional just war theory.

Deterrence as an Extreme Emergency Outside the Bounds of Just War Theory

A third major attempt by a just war theorist to justify deterrence is by Michael Walzer. Walzer recognizes more clearly than any of the others that deterrence cannot be justified by just war theory.

Walzer's description of deterrence is very optimistic. He sees it as a so far bloodless strategy which is easy to live with because it accomplishes so much with so little cost. Nevertheless, Walzer says deterrence "... is immoral. The immorality lies in the threat itself, not in its present or even its likely consequences... It is a commitment to murder."[44]

According to Walzer, a policy of counterforce cannot solve the problem because "the new technology of war doesn't fit and cannot be made to fit within the old limits."[45] Even in strict counterforce warfare, the collateral damage would be disproportionate and, in any case, the formal limits of counterforce war would almost certainly not be observed.

Walzer's critique of Ramsey is decisive. He also implicitly condemns Hehir's separation of threat and intent although his own position is the same as Hehir's in practice. He says the bomb,

> ... is designed to kill whole populations and its deterrent value depends upon that fact, (whether the killing is direct or indirect)... And men and women are responsible for the threats they live by, even if they don't speak them out loud... Unless we give up nuclear deterrence, we cannot give up such threats, and it is best that we acknowledge what it is we are doing. The real ambiguity of nuclear deterrence lies in the fact that no one, including ourselves can be sure that we will ever carry out the threats we make.[46]

In spite of the immorality of deterrence, Walzer says we cannot give it up. We cannot give it up because the values it defends cannot be relinquished. These values are the core basis of *jus ad bellum*. Walzer's argument implies a recognition that if *jus in bello* is observed then deterrence must be given up and if deterrence is abandoned, *jus ad bellum* will be lost. Defense without deterrence is impossible. Therefore victory within the boundaries of *jus in bello* is impossible. Walzer says,

> ...We see appeasement or surrender to involve a loss of values central to our existence as an independent nation-state. For it is not tolerable that advances in technology should put our nation, or any nation, at the

mercy of a great power willing to menace the world or to press its authority outwards in the shadow of an implicit threat.[47]

The implication is that the moral limits of war embedded in *jus in bello*, must be given up in order to preserve the right of self- defense.

Against an enemy actually willing to use the bomb, self-defense is impossible, and it makes sense to say that the only compensating step is the (immoral) threat to respond in kind. No country capable of making such a threat is likely to refuse to make it. What is not tolerable will not be tolerated.[48]

There are three claims implicit in Walzer's position. One is that the ability of the United States to resist Soviet aggression is a higher moral value than the preservation of consistency in just war theory. In the abstract this may be true. Logical and moral systems do not exist in a void. They must interact with their consequences. But the acceptance or rejection of a moral system affects the nature of the parties involved and the types of solutions that may become possible. Walzer's pessimism about deterrence and just war theory further assumes that nuclear deterrence is the only possible way to resist Soviet aggression.

Another claim is that the threat to do massive evil is not as bad as actually doing it and if the threat can prevent the actuality, we must threaten it, even if it is evil. Thus he says, "We threaten evil in order not to do it and the doing of it would be so terrible that the threat seems in comparison to be morally defensible."[49] This quotable sentence is a little misleading since the threat is not intended to stop ourselves but stop the Soviet Union. The threat increases the danger of *our* performing it. Morally, we are far more responsible for our actions than those of the Soviet Union.

The third implicit claim in Walzer's position is that it is politically impossible for a nation to give up the deterrent threat when the threat is the only means of defense. Walzer's argument is that with nuclear weapons true necessity has intervened and forced a nation to resort to immoral means because its very survival is at stake. Nuclear weapons have created a permanent supreme emergency.

Walzer's category of supreme emergency was created to explain extreme emergencies in rare cases where just war theory must be violated for higher ends. What happens when supreme emergency becomes an everyday permanent reality? Walzer does not shrink from the inevitable conclusion:

> Nuclear weapons explode the theory of just war. They are the first of man's technological innovations that are simply not encompassable within the familiar moral world. Or rather, our familiar notions about *jus in bello* require us to condemn even the threat to use them. And yet there are other notions also familiar, having to do with aggression and the right of self-defense, that seem to require exactly that threat. So we move uneasily beyond the limits of justice for the sake of justice (and peace).[50]

Nuclear weapons explode just war theory because with them either *jus ad bellum* or *jus in bello* must be given up. Walzer chooses to give up *jus in bello* in the case of deterrence and support the right of defense in spite of the possible consequences. His position bears a family resemblance to Augustine who was impressed with the horror of war yet could not give up the right of defense.

The other option is to give up *jus ad bellum* and accept the consequences of defenselessness. Walzer cannot accept those consequences partly because they are politically impossible. As long as the Soviet Union continues to display aggressive behavior and possess nuclear weapons it is practically impossible to conceive of the United States giving up nuclear weapons.

The prototype war that underlies Walzer's whole just war theory, is war as resistance to a genocidal power such as Hitler in relation to the Jews. Throughout Walzer's book, the spectre of defeat that is pictured is the spectre of a Hitler or a Stalin without opposition. Walzer does not believe that evil powers can be tamed by anything less than all out resistance. Ultimately Walzer does not believe that there can be any limits to a war against a force like Nazism. He says,

... it is possible to live in a world where individuals are sometimes murdered, but a world where entire peoples are enslaved or massacred is literally unbearable. Challenges such as Nazism...bring us under the rule of necessity (and necessity knows no rules).[51]

For Walzer the right of just defense cannot be given up, even if it means the end of just war theory. These are powerful thoughts which challenge the superficiality of those who assume that only irrational fear and a suicidal arms race prevents the United States and the Soviet Union from living in harmony with each other.

On the other hand, to picture U.S./Soviet nuclear competition as a type of Allied resistance to Nazism may be even more dangerous. Compromise with the Soviet Union is often referred to as analogous to appeasement at Munich. Yet there are at least three major differences. Firstly, the Soviet Union is not Nazi Germany, even if it is an oppressive system. The Soviet Union could never succeed in dominating the world in the way that Hitler envisaged it, even if they had unimpeded military power and wished to do so.[52] Secondly, a nuclear war would probably be far more disastrous than Soviet domination, even if the Soviets were as bad as the Nazis. That was not the case at Munich. And thirdly, the Munich analogy deceptively increases polarization and ignores the tremendous incentives that exist for both sides to maintain peace.

Nuclear war is not a subset of a war of defense against aggression. Perhaps the most dangerous tendency is to think of nuclear war in the same way as we think of conventional wars in the past. If the demise of just war theory forces us to choose between *jus ad bellum* and *jus in bello*, let us not choose on the basis of obsolete images of war. Deterrence institutionalizes a means of defense that outrages the assumptions of just war theory. As George Kennan remarked,

If we must defend our homes we should do so as well as we can do in the direct sense but we ought never to take part in making millions of women and children and non-combatants hostages for the behavior of their governments... It will be said to me: This means defeat. To this I can only reply: I am skeptical of the meaning of 'victory' and defeat in their relation to modern war between great countries. To my mind the defeat is war itself. In any case it seems to me that there are times when we have no choice but to follow the dictates of our conscience, to throw ourselves on God's mercy, and not ask too many questions.[53]

Two questions which we must address will be taken up in Chapter Six: To what extent can any government be expected to "throw itself on God's mercy?" And, what difference does that make for Christian ethics?

Conclusion

Just war theory is based on a mode of moral reasoning in which the justifiability of war is measured by weighing the values to be gained and lost. The proportionate reasoning of just war theory is concerned with protecting the innocent. That kind of moral thought is of permanent value. We all struggle with choices between greater and lesser evils. This is no less true for the pacifist than the non-pacifist. Proportionate reason and concern for the innocent remain central factors in any discussion of conflict in international relations.

A key turning point in this mode of reasoning involves how much weight is given to the value of defense against tyranny. There are historical circumstances in which it is necessary to physically resist, no matter how futile the cause. The systematic slaughter of the Jews in the Warsaw Ghetto provoked a resistance which was both heroic and morally necessary.

As Thomas Merton, who is known for his pacifism, said,

In practice, where non-violent resistance is impossible, then violent resistance must be used rather than passive acquiescence... Merely passive acquiescence in evil is in no sense to be dignified by the name of non-violence. It is a travesty of Christian meekness. It is purely and simply the sin of cowardice.[54]

At the extremity of necessity, when the criminal burden of

war is forced upon a conscience, the ruling factors of proportionality and concern for the innocent must be retained. A major war between great powers today could never meet the requirements of concern for the innocent and proportionate good, even if nuclear weapons were not used.

It is a long road from specific, proportionate defense against the slaughter of one's community to strategic nuclear warfare for abstract political objectives. Unfortunately, it is not possible to erect abstract road signs that can tell how far it is permissible to go along the road. *Jus ad bellum* and *jus in bello* rules attempt to tell us, but they have been defeated by the history of warfare.

The turning point of just war reasoning is the decision whether or not to make the right of just defense an absolute right, a *prima facie* right or an exceptional permission. In a world with nuclear weapons the most dangerous step is to make of defense an absolute right. One may assume that defense is a *prima facie* right and still come out a nuclear pacifist. However, as a Christian who takes the life and teachings of Jesus seriously, I believe that the most that can be said is that defense of others may be an exceptional permission.

Ramsey, Johnson, Hehir and Walzer all begin with current political and technological realities and attempt to fit them into the moral framework of the just war tradition. Their attempts fail because ultimately they give current realities a greater moral weight than any transcendent ideals.

The seven traditional categories of *jus ad bellum* attempt to provide a definitive general answer to the question of when war is justifiable. These criteria suffer from an inherent subjectivity, and a lack of consensus about their content. Ultimately they fail because they assume a different meaning to war than the reality we face today. Just war rules further the illusion that the nature of war is unchanged by nuclear technology and that the necessity of defense is an absolute right.

The rules of *jus ad bellum* cannot provide guidance on the central question of deterrence or the related question of how much risk of nuclear war is acceptable. An emphasis on the rules of *jus ad bellum* can be used to promote an ideological war similar to Cicero's just war of conquest or Harold O. J. Brown's justification of all-out war against atheistic communism. War of this type has no rational or moral place in a nuclear age. Even the most basic of human rights and states rights could not be sustained by a nuclear war.

We have noted that the greatest problem with just war theory is the tension between *jus ad bellum* and *jus in bello.*

In extreme situations the teleological reasoning of *jus ad bellum* comes into conflict with the deontological principle of discrimination.

In a war between great powers it is no longer possible for a nation that adheres to *jus in bello* to gain victory over one that does not. In modern war, *jus in bello* renders *jus ad bellum* impossible. None of the attempts to resolve this problem and retain just war theory can succeed. Nuclear weapons have clarified the irreducible tension between consequentialist and absolutist modes of reasoning in just war theory.

Discrimination is often considered the foundation of secularized just war theory and of many laudable international war conventions. Yet the foundation of discrimination (protection of the innocent) has been undercut by the nature of modern war. Discrimination is still an excellent and useful rule but its logical basis as deontological protection of the innocent has been undercut by the difficulty of equating innocence with non-combatancy, or guilt with combatancy.

The central strategic issue in the nuclear age is the problem of nuclear deterrence. Deterrence in peace time does not fit under holocaust, whether counterforce or countervalue, appears to be the only means of military defense. Yet it massively violates the assumptions of just warfare. Just war theory as a set of rules cannot address the problem of deterrence.

Ramsey's attempt to find a justifiable use for nuclear weapons in counterforce warfare results in a distortion of both just war theory and political reality. Nor can the principle of proportion have much meaning when the values to be weighed are imponderable. Ramsey's justification of the counterforce use of small nuclear weapons ignores the terrible pressure to escalate that would accompany any nuclear war over great stakes.

Both Hehir and Walzer have attempted to justify deterrence without the actual intent to use the weapons in warfare. Both continue to hope that deterrence will not fail before a better solution to the problem of defense is found.

The traditional answers of just war theory have failed because they cannot comprehend the questions that modern war asks. The *jus in bello* categories may still be useful for restricting certain types of modern war but they provide no means of calculating the risk of nuclear war latent in any war.

If just war theory is anachronistic, how can Christians decide how they and their governments should respond to the unique dangers of our age? Before we examine a Christian perspective we will first consider the wisdom and folly of political realism.

1   Robert A. Gessert, "The Case for Selective Options," in Robert
    Gessert and Bryan Hehir, *The New Nuclear Debate*, (New York:
    Council on Religion and International Affairs, 1976) is a good
    example of the counterforce position. James Douglass, *The
    Non-Violent Cross* (New York: Macmillan, 1966) represents a
    pacifist position that claims warrant from the just war tradition.

2   Michael Walzer, *Just and Unjust Wars* (New York: Basic Books,
    1977). Walzer's interest in just war theory grew out of his
    opposition to the Vietnam war.

3   James F. Childress, "Just War Criteria," in Thomas A. Shannon,
    ed. War or Peace?: The Search for New Answers (Maryknoll,
    NY: Orbis, 1980), p. 41-41.

4   William K. Frankena, *Ethics*, 2nd Ed. (Englewood Cliffs, NJ:
    Prentice-Hall, 1973), pp. 41-42.

5   Childress, "Just War Criteria," p. 49.

6   Michael Walzer, *Just and Unjust Wars*, p. 15.

7   Ibid., p. 19.

8   Ibid., p. 54.

9   Ibid., p. 67.

10 Paul Ramsey, *War and the Christian Conscience* (Durham, NC:
    Duke University Press, 1961), p. 9.

11 Harold O.J. Brown, "Rumors of War," *Eternity*,(June, 1980), pp.
    16-17.

12 John Courtney Murray, "Remarks on the Moral Problem of
    War," *Theological Studies* XX, 1, (March, 1959).

13 Ibid., p. 52. Cf. Ramsey, p. 136. The most able recent statement of
    this position is by James Turner Johnson, *Can Modern Wars Be
    Just?* New Haven (Yale University Press, 1984).

14 This statement is worthy of a separate chapter or at least a few
    pages. It assumes a notion of human rights, some sort of social
    contract doctrine, and a conception of international society. I am
    in general agreement with Michael Walzer's discussion of these
    terms; *Just and Unjust Wars*, ch. 4, "Law and Order in
    International Society," pp. 51-73. I do not agree with his
    statement, in this section, that "the deepest purpose of a state is
    defense" (p. 59). As I have already indicated, I also cannot agree
    with his unmodified statement that, "In just war doctrine, as in
    the legalist paradigm, the triumph of aggression is a greater evil
    than the outbreak of war" (p. 68). The deepest purpose of a state
    is not a static concept that underlies all else. The purpose of a
    state changes with historical circumstances. Even in war-time
    the "deepest purpose of a state" may be to surrender or to
    restrain the possible level of defense. A significant flaw in

Walzer's very fine book is that his basic image of war is one of defense against annihilation along the lines of the Jewish Holocaust. This prototype must be reckoned with, especially by pacifists; but it is not the primary historical form of warfare, nor is it the most useful way to think about nuclear warfare.

15 Earlier forms of this principle included other just causes, such as the righting of wrongs. Modern just war theory reduces it to defense.

16 See for example Ralph B. Potter, *War and Moral Discourse* (Richmond, VA: John Knox Press), 1969.

17 Ibid., p. 21. Just and Unjust Wars, p. 21.

18 Carl Von Clausewitz, *On War,* Michael Howard and Peter Paret, eds. & trans. (Princeton, NJ: Princeton University Press, 1976), p. 76.

19 Ramsey, *Christian Conscience,* p. 168.

20 Ibid., pp. 192-198.

21 Ibid., p. xxii.

22 Walzer, p. 260.

23 Ibid., p. 268.

24 *Can Modern War be Just?*, pp. 16-17.

25 Ibid., p. 32.

26 Ibid., p. 40. cf. p. 29.

27 Ibid., p. 39. cf. pp. 35-47.

28 Ibid., p. 69.

29 Ibid., p. 71.

30 Ibid., p. 85.

31 Ibid., p. 78.

32 Ibid., p. 189.

33 Ibid., p. 76.

34 John C. Ford, S.J., "The Morality of Obliteration Bombing." *Theological Studies,* 5 (1944), reprinted in Richard A. Wasserstrom, ed., *War and Morality* (Belmont, CA: Wadsworth, 1970). See also Elizabeth Anscombe, "War and Murder," ibid., pp. 42-53.

35 Some writers such as Elizabeth Anscombe, ibid., show their discomfort with the term guilt as applied to drafted combatants by using the term "non-innocence." The effect is the same. Whether reluctant draftees are labeled "guilty" or non-innocent they are still killed for the sins of their government.

36 Michael Walzer, "Moral Judgement in Time of War," in Wasserstrom, ed., *War and Morality,* p. 58.

37 See James Turner Johnson, *Reason, Ideology and the Limitation of War: Religious and Secular Concepts, 1200-1740* (Princeton:

Princeton University Press, 1975).

38 Ramsey, *Christian Conscience,* p. 11, p. 239.

39 Paul Ramsey, *The Just War* (New York: Charles Scribner's Sons, 1968), p. 254.

40 Ramsey has been the subject of extensive critical discussion. A measure of his importance is indicated by the fact that almost every recent book on war and morality includes a section or chapter on Ramsey's thought. At least one published dissertation is devoted solely to a discussion of Ramsey's just war theory.   Ernest Ruede, OFM CONV., *The Morality of War* (Rome: Pontifica Universitas Lateranensis, 1970). Notable other critiques include James W. Douglass, *The Non-Violent Cross* (New York: MacMillan, 1966), pp. 55- 121; Walzer, *Just and Unjust Wars,* pp. 270-272, 278-283; Frederick O. Bonkovsky, *International Norms and National Policy* (Grand Rapids, Mich.: Wm. B. Eerdmans, 1980), pp. 119-136.

41 J. Bryan Hehir, "The Just War Ethic and Catholic Theology: Dynamics of Change and Continuity" in Shannon, pp. 15-39.

42 Gessert and Hehir, *New Nuclear Debate,* p. 50. This position is echoed by Kenneth Waltz, *The Spread of Nuclear Weapons: More May Be Better,* Adelphi Paper. No. 171 (London: The International Institute for Strategic Studies, 1981), p.24.

43 Ibid., p. 50.

44 Walzer, *Just and Unjust Wars,* p. 271.

45 Ibid., p. 276.

46 Ibid., pp. 281-282. Walzer's statement that people "are responsible for the threats they live by, even if they don't speak them out loud," also undercuts the attempt to separate possession of nuclear weapons from the threat to use them. Possession of nuclear weapons apart from a spoken threat is only useful insofar as an unspoken threat is understood. Thus Winter's suggestion that "Mere Possession of the strategic arsenal as a deterrent is morally neutral," cannot be maintained if the spoken threat is condemned. See Francis X. Winters, "The Bow or the Cloud?" *America,* July 25, 1981, p. 28.

47 Walzer, Just and Unjust Wars, p. 273.

48 Ibid., p. 274.

49 Ibid.

50 Ibid., p. 282.

51 Ibid., p. 254.

52 While the Soviets retain their rigid ideological rhetoric, the revolutionary dynamism that characterized early communism is no longer there. See John C. Bennett, "Soviet Aims and

Priorities: The Need for a New Debate," *Christianity and Crisis,* October 19, 1981. pp. 275-279. See also George F. Kennan, "U.S.-Soviet Relations: Turning from Catastrophe," *Christianity and Crisis,* May 26, 1980, pp. 155-158.

53 George F. Kennan in an address at Princeton University. Quoted in Paul Ramsey, *Christian Conscience,* pp. 157-158.

54 Thomas Merton, *On Peace* (New York: McCall, 1971), p. 104.

CHAPTER V

THE WISDOM AND FOLLY OF
POLITICAL REALISM

The breakdown of just war theory raises the question of whether morality is even relevant to the unique problems of modern war. The hazards of moralism have led many political scientists to abandon the task of moral evaluation in international politics. Instead they attempt to describe, explain and, if possible, predict the relations of states to one another. Ethical analysis is avoided because of suspicion, bordering on conviction, that moral issues have no concrete meaning in international relations. Behavior of states is thought to be determined by the necessity of survival or perceived national interest.

It has often been suggested that the problems of international relations (including the problem of nuclear weapons), are not moral problems at all, but technical problems. Nations do not, according to this view, follow moral principles except when it is in their own interest to do so. An article by Werner Levi expresses a common perception of the relation between ethics and international politics. The article is titled, "The Relative Irrelevance of Moral Norms in International Relations."[1] Levi argues that while moral norms do influence policy makers, whenever norms conflict with interests, interests overrule.

Kenneth W. Thompson reaches a similar conclusion regarding nuclear weapons. Thompson points out that everyone agrees that nuclear war is terrible. Since the prevailing view of nuclear war is the same for militarists and moralists alike, what is the point of moralizing about it? Preventing nuclear war is a technical military problem of maintaining a balance of power. An emphasis on ethics may simply make the problem more difficult.[2] Both of these authors reflect a major approach to international problems that is known as "political realism."

The first section of this chapter defines political realism

by discussing some of the major classics of international relations theory. The great realist thinkers of the past developed a set of concepts and metaphors that continue to influence the way political scientists perceive the problem of conflict in international politics.

The second section considers a modern realist who utilizes and extends the classical realist concepts to explain modern international behavior. Kenneth Waltz is chosen to illustrate modern realism because he is possibly the most scientifically rigorous and internally consistent realist writer to date. Waltz is also interesting because he employs a structural theory that suggests that there are immutable laws of international behavior.

The third section provides an ethical critique of systems theory in general and Waltz's theory in particular.

The fourth section examines the meaning of four central "metaphors" that form the basis of realism.

In section five, we see that military power is no longer the means of security and dominance that it once was.

Section six examines the perspective on nuclear war that Kenneth Waltz draws from structural realism.

A Historical Definition of Political Realism

Realism may be defined in terms of a stream of political reasoning about international relations traceable from Niccolo Machiavelli through Thomas Hobbes, Jean Jacques Rousseau and Friedrich Meinecke. The ideas and metaphors provided by those authors have become firmly entrenched in the discipline of international relations theory. While relatively few political scientists explicitly espouse classical realist theory, almost all incorporate at least some of the major insights of political realism into their basic assumptions about international relations. For many scholars, political realism is equivalent to political science. The dominant metaphors of realism have deeply informed their perception of reality.

Niccolo Machiavelli

Machiavelli argued that politics and international relations should be a descriptive and explanatory science rather than a branch of moral philosophy.[3] Realist political science is not intended to prescribe how states should related so much as to describe and explain how they do in fact relate to each other. Machiavelli's desire to get closer to political reality suggests that there is a profound gap between the conventional morality that politicians profess, and the way in which successful politicians operate. Machiavelli's major insight is that politics is a competition for power. Successful politics require the judicious use of power without any moral restrictions beyond the requirements of utility. Utility is defined in terms of material self-interest.

Thomas Hobbes

Thomas Hobbes introduced the idea of basic reality as an "anarchic state of nature" in which law has no meaning. Hobbes suggested that conflict is caused by three factors: competition, diffidence (i.e. lack of trust), and glory. Thus war occurs for gain, for safety and for reputation. In the state of nature, Hobbes concluded in his famous lines, there is "... continual fear, and danger of violent death, and the life of man (is) solitary, poor, nasty, brutish and short."[4]

For Hobbes, the state of nature is not just a hypothetical construct. He saw it as the historical precursor to the formation of a civil state. Hobbes suggested that the state of nature still exists in primitive areas of the world. The civil state is the result of a social contract in which people create an artificial person, a leviathan, to escape the intolerable insecurity of the state of nature.

With the creation of this artificial person (i.e. the state), people give up their liberty to secure their own interests by any means within their power. In return the state promises a certain degree of security. Hobbes believed that the state must be very powerful to restrain the state of nature.

Hobbes pointed out that in international relations there is

no social contract and no artificial authority to provide security for states. States are in a perpetual state of nature with each other and the law of the jungle prevails. In the international state of nature:

> ... kings and persons of sovereign authority, because of their independency, are in continual jealousies, and in the state and posture of gladiators, having their weapons pointing, and their eyes fixed on one another; that is, their forts, garrisons and guns upon the frontiers of their kingdoms, and continual spies upon their neighbors, which is a posture of war.[5]

Hobbes understood morality to be contingent upon a social contract. Ethical values have no meaning in a state of nature where there is no mediating authority to ensure reciprocity. Unlike Machiavelli, Hobbes felt that within the bounds of a social contract there is meaning to natural law. But like Machiavelli and the modern realists for whom Hobbes is the prototype, law and justice have no meaning in the international state of nature.

> To this war of every man against every man, this also is consequent; that nothing can be unjust. The notions of right and wrong, justice and injustice, here have no common place; where there is no common power, there is no law; where no law, no injustice.[6]

For Hobbes, the laws of nature are derived from reason and aim to achieve peace. But without a social contract the laws of reason can have no concrete meaning. In international relations all that is left is the right of nature: to take care of oneself in any way possible.

Thus, the "security dilemma" arises; a perceived reality of international relations in which every nation is forced to ultimately rely on its own wits and strength to survive. There is no external authority which can guarantee security in the anarchic realm of international relations.

Jean-Jacques Rousseau

Jean-Jacques Rousseau provided a structural explanation for the state of nature which explained the security dilemma without reference to the morality or nature of the governments involved. Even the most ideal government that embodied the "general will" or the "common good" of its citizens would only embody a "particular will" in relation to other states. Thus the "national interest" of even an ideal state is bound to clash with the interest of other states and result in conflict.

In an anarchic realm where survival is at stake, "self-help" is understood to be necessary, irrespective of morality. Unlike Hobbes, for whom the security dilemma was a triumph of the non- rational over the rational, Rousseau believed that the security dilemma was the simple result of states pursuing their own national self-interest in a realm that is without governing authority.[7] For Rousseau, and many others since, the only solution to the security dilemma would be a strong world government capable of enforcing on all nations the laws it made.

Rousseau attempted to show the inevitability of particular wills clashing, even if they have completely rational motivations, through his metaphor of the stag hunt. The stag hunt metaphor pictures five people who are starving and agree to hunt a stag. One sees a chance to catch a hare and grabs it thereby allowing the stag to escape. Thus an individual's immediate self-interest takes rational precedence over the interests of the group.

In the anarchic international system, a voluntary federation of states cannot work, according to Rousseau, no matter how virtuous the states. There will always be conflicts of interest that prevent or undermine cooperation. The only true solution is an international social contract backed up by a strong centralized government analogous to the governments of states.

> The Federation must embrace all the important Powers in its membership; it must have a legislative Body with powers to pass laws and ordinances binding upon all its members; it must have a coercive force capable of

compelling every state to obey its common resolves whether in the way of command or of prohibition; finally it must be strong and firm enough to make it impossible for any member to withdraw at his own pleasure the moment he conceives his private interest to clash with that of the whole body.[8]

Without a world government, Rousseau believed that the world would continue to be characterized by an uneasy balance of power with various outbreaks of war.

Friedrich Meinecke

Friedrich Meinecke furthered this stream of thought by systematically expounding Hegel's belief that the state's highest duty is its own preservation. For Hegel a state lives by a different and higher morality than individuals.[9] Meinecke developed the concept of autonomous political morality by use of the concept of *raison d'etat*. *Raison d'etat*, according to Meinecke, requires that conventional law and morality be ignored when they do not further the good of the state. *Raison d'etat* provides the justification for *realpolitik*. For Meinecke any action in international relations can be justified if it furthers the national interest. *Raison d'etat* incorporates all the central aspirations of human culture. The state is the highest value.

The single major result of the realist metaphors is the "balance of power." According to classical realism all nations seek power in order to preserve their own security. While the term "balance of power" is relatively new, realists claim that power balancing has always characterized international relations. If nations in the state of nature do not destroy each other, it is because the power of each state is balanced by the others. This idea was implicitly recognized by Thucydides in ancient Greece and Kautilya in ancient India.[10] David Hume thought the concept was self-evident. He said,

... the maxim of preserving the balance of power if founded so much on common sense and obvious reasoning, that it is impossible it could altogether have escaped antiquity.[11]

The Realist-Idealist Debate

The term "realism" would be a pale truism with no concrete meaning if it were not for its historical definition in opposition to "idealism." Realism is not distinguished from idealism on a moral basis. Realists such as Reinhold Neibuhr are highly concerned about morality while some Marxist idealists profess little interest in morality.

The basic difference between the two concerns the fundamental nature of political reality. The idealists of the 1930s and 1940s often emphasized how nations ought to behave and rejected the way nations did behave as simply wrong. According to Dougherty and Pfaltzgraff,

> ... the American utopians disdained balance of power politics... national armaments, the use of force in international affairs and the secret treaties of alliance and spoils division attendant on World War I. Instead they stressed international legal rights and obligations, the natural harmony of national interests—reminiscent of Adam Smith's 'invisible hand'—as a regulation for the preservation of international peace, a heavy reliance upon reason in human affairs, and confidence in the peace building function of the 'world court of public opinion.'[12]

In the 1940s a virulent debate took place between "realists" and "idealists." Realism and idealism are ideal types. There will always be some elements of both in serious theories. But the weight of history in the above debate was clearly on the side of the realists. E.H. Carr commented on the debate that, "the inner meaning of the modern international crisis is the collapse of the whole structure of utopianism based on the concept of the harmony of interests."[13] World War II effectively shut off the realist-idealist debate.

These then are the dominant concepts and metaphors of realism. International relations is an "anarchic realm" where the only law is the law of survival, i.e., "the state of nature." This gives rise to the "security dilemma" which requires that each state seek its own "national interest" guided only by its *"raison d'etat."* The behavior of states in international affairs is thus characterized by *realpolitik* in a "self-help system."

The result, both in strategy and in practice is a "balance of power."

Kenneth Waltz illustrates how these terms are used among some political scientists today.

Realism Linked to International Structures: Kenneth Waltz

Some realists derive their theory from a particular understanding of human nature. This has always troubled political scientists who wish to exclude such "philosophical speculations" from social science. Structural theory attempts to exclude ethical and philosophical ideas and build a theory that will explain interstate behavior irrespective of the characteristics of its main actors.

Kenneth Waltz has probably produced the most carefully reasoned version of structural realism.[14] Waltz contrasts balance of power theory with *Realpolitik* and the international structure. *Realpolitik,* defined in terms of interests and necessity, indicates the methods by which international politics are conducted. Structural constraints describe why these methods are repeatedly used in spite of differences in actors. Balance of power theory explains the result such methods produce.

Balance of power begins with several assumptions: states are unitary actors which minimally seek their own preservation and maximally strive for world domination by means of internal efforts such as increasing military capability or by means of external efforts such as enlarging their alliances.[15] These assumptions are theoretical simplifications. They are not intended to be descriptive of the complexity of real history.

Following from these assumptions, Waltz suggests only two conditions are needed for a balance of power to form and operate in international politics: two or more states must co-exist in a self- help system.[16] A self-help system is one in which each state can ultimately count on nothing but its own wits to insure its survival. In Hobbesian terms, international politics are in a state of nature where fear governs life because of competition, desire for glory and diffidence.

Waltz believes that fear of failure in a self-help system stimulates states to behave in ways that tend towards balance of power. Thus balance of power is a condition, or idealized state of affairs that is explained by balance of power theory. It does not depend on rationality or any particular strategy. Power balancing may or may not be a good conscious strategy. Balance of power does not depend on states accepting its "rules." Rather, it is the result towards which a self-help system tends.

Waltz argues that balance of power theory cannot be expected to explain every particular situation. That, he suggests, would be like expecting the law of universal gravitation to explain the path of a falling leaf. Theory explains tendencies and constraints, not necessarily specific situation.

Nevertheless, Waltz suggests that balance of power politics prevail wherever two and only two requirements are met: 1) the order is anarchic, and 2) the units wish to survive.[17] If these conditions are met, then in theory the good or bad motives of states cannot result in anything but a balance of power.

Balance of power theory does not suggest that if accepted it will bring peace. On the contrary, the standard realist assumption is that the state of nature in international structure is a state of war, at least in the sense of war as a constant threat. Hans Morgenthau argued that power balancing as a strategy reduces the likelihood of war. Waltz's theory suggests that even if all states accepted the theory and used it consistently as a strategy, wars would probably still occur. Waltz's theory does not predict the behavior of individual states or particular leaders. Rather, he suggests, it influences and constrains actors in certain directions whether or not they "believe" in it. According to the theory, states who do not balance power will not survive as major actors in the system. States that do balance power may or may not have peace.

In a self-help system the ruling assumption, according to

Waltz, is Machiavelli's insight that utility fundamentally governs behavior for survival. Other values are subsumed to utility not necessarily by choice but by necessity. Those who do not follow the "rules" of competition and socialization simply do not survive.

An Ethical Critique of Structural Realism

Waltz's theory begins with a definition of the international system, (that it is anarchic), and ends with an explanation of why states behave the way they do. Waltz is more careful than most system theorists in distinguishing between theory and reality. A theory, according to Waltz, should not attempt to describe reality but to explain it. An explanation necessarily abstracts from reality elements considered key determinants of the system. The system is based on a model of international relations that is considered an oversimplified but accurate representation of reality.

Waltz's thesis is that the structure of the system of international politics determines the long term behavior of the units in the system. In Waltz's model of the system, his reasoning is internally consistent and very convincing. In a self-help, anarchic, segmentary system in which fear governs life, one would expect surviving units to move towards some kind of balance of power. The problem with Waltz's theory is not in the internal consistency of his model but in the relation between the model and reality.

One cannot prove false Waltz's theory by pointing out empirical historical facts that do not fit into his model. His model is not meant to explain all facts or all behavior. Waltz does not deny that units have a measure of freedom to act against the constraints of the structure. But his theory requires that the structure is ultimately determinative. Units that do not follow the dictates of self-help will eventually not survive, at least not as central actors in the system.

In spite of Waltz's careful distinction between his model and reality, it is clear that unless his model accurately portrays the central determining factors in interstate behavior, it cannot provide an explanation of reality. Unless there really is a system of international relations that has a structure like the one in Waltz's model, his model is misleading. Waltz realizes that reality is extremely complex but he believes that the most important determinants of real interstate behavior are included in his model.

Because Waltz believes there is a determining structure in the international system of states, there is little room for morality in international relations. States and politicians do not have the freedom to choose to act in a way that does not further their national interest. Part of a definition of morality includes the freedom to act against selfishness and even against self-interest on the basis of transcendent values. But in Waltz's system selfish behavior is requisite. In the state of nature, states are in a kind of eternal dance in which the same steps are repeated over and over again. Balance of power theory explains the structure of the dance.

In Waltz's theory the structure of international relations is not determined by the characteristics of the units. Reinhold Niebuhr and Hans Morgenthau argued that balance of power politics was necessary because human beings are selfish and power-seeking. Structural theory argues that states seek their own selfish interests because the structure requires them to in order to survive. The structure determines behavior. States whether they like it or not, will tend toward power balancing and the "stability," "equilibrium" and "balance" of the whole.[18]

Because the structure, not the units, is dominant, the system has its own built-in teleology. No matter what the characteristics of the states, the system will tend towards a balance of power.

Thus Waltz suggests that the Cold War is not primarily the result of ideological conflict between the U.S. and the U.S.S.R.. It is simply the natural balancing behavior of two great powers that face each other in the state of nature.

The notion of balance or equilibrium is an isomorphism drawn from the physical sciences. Many sciences utilize the idea of equilibrium. In chemistry, solutions may be described as in a state of stable equilibrium; economists speak of a balance between supply and demand; ecologists describe the balance of nature; in national politics the idea of checks and balances is common.[19] Thus the idea of a balance of power among nations as a goal of international structure is intuitively reasonable.

The meaning of balance of power is uncertain. Ernst B. Haas found eight separate meanings of the term in the literature of international relations theory:

  a.) Any distribution of power;
  b.) an equilibrium or balancing process;
  c.) hegemony or the search for hegemony;
  d.) stability and peace in a concert of power;
  e.) instability and war;
  f.) power politics in general;
  g.) a universal law of history; and
  h.) a system and guide to policy makers.[20]

Waltz narrows the meaning of balance of power. In his theory it is primarily an equilibrium or balancing process that is a natural outcome of a segmentary system. But the precise meaning is still an intuitive abstraction that can be applied to widely differing phenomena. Almost any configuration of states could be termed a balance.

As a theoretical state of affairs, balance of power explains some actions in international politics. The arms race is an obvious example. But as a master variable that dominates all other variables, balance of power depends on the judgement that all other concepts of Waltz's structural theory accurately describe the primary factors in international politics. Waltz's modest statement that a structural theory only describes the pressures states face, not the way they will react to the pressures, obscures the fact that Waltz believes the pressures are ultimately determinative.

Structural theory is descriptive of some of the pressures in international relations. But it moves beyond description to implicit prescription backed by value judgments when it assumes these pressures are determinative. Waltz denies that the balance of power theory is normative. Thus he agrees with Nadel who says, "... an orderliness abstracted from behavior cannot guide behavior."[21] But Waltz's theory is much more than "an orderliness abstracted from behavior." While Nadel only claims to describe certain aspects of international structure, Waltz deterministically explains why the structure will always tend towards a balance of power. Nadel produces a "statistical model."[22] Waltz argues for a universal theory.

Waltz's theory does indicate a set of values and a normative policy direction. If Waltz's analysis of international structure is requisite then *realpolitik* is also requisite. If assertion of power against power is necessary and inevitable then there cannot be anything morally wrong with it. If national interests and necessity are always the ultimate or dominant determiners of international behavior, values that contradict them are ultimately "non- functional" or suicidal.

Realist theory not only describes elements in the structure of international relations, it assumes that they are necessarily the dominant factors in state behavior.

Problems with the Dominant Metaphors of Realism

Realist concepts and metaphors are all evocative, value laden interpretations of international political behavior. Although they indicate an aspect of political reality that has a powerful influence on behavior, they do not describe all aspects of the structure of political relationships. In fact, there are other metaphors that describe other structural aspects of international behavior.

To choose one set of metaphors over another as the determinative structure cannot be done on empirical grounds. Reality is far more complex than any metaphor. Any picture of reality that is drawn includes assumptions about human history, value and purpose, not because the elements of the picture are fabricated out of nothing, but because out of an infinite number of facts, a few specific facts were chosen to indicate a simple abstract picture. The simple picture may or may not provide the most significant explanation of the structure of reality. But it necessarily reflects the moral and philosophical perceptions of its author.

The State of Nature

The "State of Nature" is a good example of a selective and subjective concept of reality. Hobbes and Rousseau differed profoundly over the significance of the original metaphor. Hobbes saw the state of nature as a frightening war of all against all. Rousseau understood original nature as an ideal state of individualistic self-sufficiency. Hobbes saw socialization and the institution of autocratic government as a solution to the state of nature while Rousseau saw socialization as the root of conflict, and government as the basis of oppression. They both agreed that international relations was a state of war, but not as to the meaning of "nature."

Is conflict "natural" or is "co-operation?" Is war a "natural" state with peace only a hard-earned respite? Or is peace the "natural" state with war an unfortunate breakdown? Realists stake their theory on the naturalness of war in an anarchic system. Others, like Margaret Mead and Eric Fromm argue that war is a learned trait that can be unlearned.

These are profound epistomological questions that have no specific answer. The word "nature" cannot be pinned down with respect to human behavior. Descriptively all political behavior is "natural." There are both co-operative and belligerent relationships between nations that cannot be defined by material self interest. The Middle East provides examples of both. Relationships among nations are "natural" in the sense that they exist. But the "state of nature" in those relationships is not normative and the future is indeterminate.

The Anarchic Self-Help Realm

Another realist metaphor is that of an "anarchic, self-help realm." Anarchy can be taken as a simple descriptive term. There is, in fact, no human ruler over the nations. But anarchy is an emotion charged word. It connotes disorder, violence and fear. "Self-help" indicates that one cannot trust anyone. Because there is no ruler, no law, each state must depend on its own strength and wits to survive.

Fear, distrust, disorder and precariousness do characterize international relations. But anarchy and self-help are only two factors among many in international politics. They are certainly not literal descriptions. The degree to which they are decisive factors in international relations is a matter of great debate. The lack of a powerful world ruler and an enforceable law is taken by realist theory to ensure continual conflict. Realists have assumed that rational self-preservation in an arena of lawless power requires the use of equally lawless power. However, "the arena of lawless power" is not necessarily or always the most significant picture of international relations.

The rhetoric of interdependence and natural harmony of interests is certainly overblown and may be even less convincing than "anarchy" as a master variable. But interdependence indicates another aspect of international relations that sometimes has greater influence on interstate behavior than anarchy. Of course reality is always more complex than any metaphor can explain. States are vast bureaucracies driven by the competition of many different interests. If anarchy is taken as a significant objective condition that is one of many influences on state behavior then I think the term is useful. But as a single master variable it is misleading.

The Security Dilemma

From the idea that international relations is an anarchic state of nature, realists derive the idea of a security dilemma. Security is clearly a central issue in international relations. In Waltz's model the security dilemma is the most significant factor in interstate behavior. In the realist ideal type, military force is considered the major source of security. Force is both usable and the most effective instrument of policy. While many issues compete for state attention, military security is understood by realists to dominate the others.

Robert Keohane and Joseph Nye suggest an alternative

ideal type labeled "complex interdependence."[23] Like realism, complex interdependence is not a literal description of international relations. Out of the innumerable facets of interstate behavior it seeks to isolate the most significant facts that influence international relations. The following assumptions of complex interdependence are chosen for their contrast with realist assumptions:

a.) Multiple channels connect society. The state is not a single coherent unit but a complex of organizations each of which has its own agenda. Moreover many non-governmental organizations connect societies, each of which exerts its own influence on governmental leaders. International relations is more like a political convention than a chess game.

b.) The agenda of international relations consists of multiple issues with no clear or consistent hierarchy. Military security does not necessarily or actually dominate the hierarchy. Between some countries and at some times military security does have priority over other issues but the hierarchy of issues is fluid. Different issues dominate at different times. As Henry Kissinger remarked in 1975, "The problems of energy, resources, environment, population, the uses of space and sea now rank with questions of military security, ideology and territorial rivalry which have traditionally made up the diplomatic agenda."[24]

The security dilemma is usually defined as a military problem. But there are a large number of issues that equally threaten the security of nation states. In the short run it is the poorer nations of the world that are most threatened by non-military catastrophe. But in the long run the superpowers cannot escape the threats of ecological deterioration and resource depletion. In 1969, United Nations Secretary U Thant said,

> I do not wish to seem overdramatic, but I can only conclude from the information that is available to me as Secretary-General, that the members of the United Nations have perhaps ten years left in which to subordinate their ancient quarrels and launch a global partnership to curb the arms race, to improve the human environment, to defuse the population explosion, and to supply the required momentum to development efforts. If

such a global partnership is not forged within the next decade, then I very much fear that the problems I have mentioned will have reached such staggering proportions that they will be beyond our capacity to control.[25]

Perhaps U Thant was overdramatic. However the problems he was referring to have not disappeared.

c.) Military force is sometimes irrelevant for solving complex issues of interdependence. On many issues force is neither usable nor effective as a tool of policy. Even among nations that are antagonistic to one another, large areas of their relationship may be immune from military influences.

Security is a very slippery term. Its most basic definition relates to people, not to states. There is both an objective and subjective meaning to security. Most simply, objective security means not being killed while subjective security means not fearing that one is about to be killed. For most people, and for states, security means a great deal more. Security is psychologically related to identity. Insofar as people locate the security of their identity in the wealth, power, virtue, prestige, influence or altruism of their nation, the preservation of those characteristics will be an important part of security.

In the realist model, the security dilemma refers to threats on the survival of the state. Other values are important but subordinate to survival. Keohane and Nye's complex interdependence does not question the fundamental value of survival but rather the relation between survival and other values, and the relation between survival and military power.

Security and survival may be the paramount value without being the dominating value. For example, I have a security dilemma every time I jaywalk across a busy street. I have a certain degree of fear and mistrust of the oncoming drivers. Moreover in relation to drivers, my paramount value is survival. Jaywalking does not cause me to give up other values or threaten with a gun any car that doesn't let me cross. The security dilemma is simply not severe enough to challenge any of my stronger values. Survival is best accomplished by avoiding the cars, cooperating with them if they slow down, or walking to a corner.

Stanley Hoffmann implies that the security dilemma is a

continuum. Thus he speaks of the "Hobbesian floor" and the "Kantian ceiling" as limits of moral interstate behavior.[26] When international relations deteriorate, the security dilemma becomes much more acute. At the Hobbesian floor there is no room for moral behavior except as it furthers immediate interests. When relations are better the possibilities of cooperative and even altruistic behavior increase.

Waltz assumes that the security dilemma is part of the structure of international relations independent of the characteristics of the states. The character and meaning of the security dilemma changes according to the relations and characteristics of the states. The security dilemma between the U.S. and China is very different from the security dilemma between the United States and the Soviet Union. It is not only that different states react differently to a uniform security dilemma. The nature of the security dilemma changes and different states respond differently.

In an age when war has become a psychological process characterized by threats and warnings that are backed by apocalyptic power, the security dilemma has also become a mental process. The objective danger of a particular threat is significantly influenced by the subjective perceptions of both opponents. For the foreseeable future, there will always be an objective security dilemma between states. The mere existence of nuclear weapons constitutes a security dilemma. The scale of danger the security dilemma represents depends on many variables, including the attitudes and perceptions of the states involved.

The psychological aspect of the security dilemma is particularly acute between two powers that each have an indisputable ability to destroy the other. If deterrence is the only defense, then security is influenced by a country's perception of its opponents ability and intent, by its perception of its own ability and by the values that are held to constitute a nation's identity. Freedom from the objective security dilemma is not possible. It cannot be bought with any number of weapons. But freedom from the dominance of the subjective security dilemma depends on the easing of tensions and the concentration on values that   transcend international competition.

In a world where genocidal weapons are a given, the realist assumption that security can be obtained through ever increasing military strength is an illusion. The continual increase in genocidal weapons cannot increase security. Whether an arms race that maintains some kind of weapons parity (or "balance") will maintain or undercut the present level of security is a matter of subjective perception. The present costs of such an arms race are great and the long-term prospects of avoiding the use of such genocidal weapons is dim.

Continuing weapons competition undermines the non-military basis of security. The arms race intensifies the security dilemma because it perpetuates the equation of security with military balance while it furthers the possibility of imbalance through technological breakthrough. The meaning of the security dilemma would change if values other than military balance or preponderance were held to constitute security. No one can predict exactly how objective security would be effected if the idea of weapons balance were abandoned. But non-military values that contribute to security would certainly be strengthened and, in the opinion of this writer, the inherent worth of those values would justify the risk.

In summary, the realist conception of the security dilemma is not a value-free explanation of state behavior. Particularly in an age of war by apocalyptic threat, the realist equation of security with military strength creates its own reality. The security dilemma is defined by each nation's acceptance of the realist conception of it. The security dilemma is an abstraction that is used to describe the real relations of states to one another. Fear and danger are objective factors in interstate relations. But how they are related to military strength is a product of how people think about them.

Raison d'Etat and Realpolitik

Raison d'etat is another abstraction in realist theory that lends itself to changing definitions. Very generally, *raison d'etat* spans the concepts of national interests and necessity. *Realpolitik* describes the policies and actions that result from *raison d'etat.* Kenneth Waltz describes the elements of *realpolitik* as follows:

> The ruler's, and later the state's interest provides the spring of action; the necessities of policy arise from the unregulated competition of states; calculation based on these necessities can discover the policies that will best serve a state's interests; success is defined as preserving and strengthening the state.[27]

It is important to once again make the distinction between these concepts as objective description, explanation or ethical prescription. Waltz's simple definition of *realpolitik* is tautological; interests and necessities determine a state's actions. The key questions are, of course, what are a state's interests? What does a state perceive as necessity? What constitutes preserving and strengthening the state? The assumptions behind *realpolitik* set it off from rival concepts. *Realpolitik* assumes that national interest is primarily concerned with political and economic power, and that necessity comes into play whenever power is threatened.

Machiavelli is the archetypal exponent of *raison d'etat* and *realpolitik.* Meinecke attempted to modify Machiavelli's monism by suggesting a dialectical approach in which both morality and power are included in the *raison d'etat.* They do not merge. *Realpolitik* cannot be restricted by morality but only by *raison d'etat,* which keeps moral ends in view. Yet Meinecke's underlying assumption is that the highest stage of human development is represented by the state. The primary means by which a state may reach its (ultimately moral) objectives is through the use of power.

Waltz does not engage in the kind of agonized discussion of power and morality that characterized Meinecke. For Waltz, *raison d'etat* and *realpolitik* are simply descriptive of the way nations behave in an anarchic system. While Meinecke treats raison d'etat as a normative concept, Waltz considers it an oversimplified or abstracted description. The actual activities of states are far too complex to fit into the terms of *raison d'etat* and *realpolitik* unless these terms are simply defined as "everything a state does."

Waltz's use of *raison d'etat* and *realpolitik* moves a step beyond description. These terms are used as abstractions which are part of a model that explains international behavior. As such they represent a particular interpretation of international behavior that assumes a   particular normative meaning to the state, its interests and its necessities. *Raison d'etat* and *realpolitik* cannot be purely descriptive expressions and explanatory concepts at the same time. As part of a theoretical model, both concepts assume that the state is its own highest value, and that the most rational, indeed the only rational way for the state to survive is to act without moral restraint according to the *raison d'etat*. For Waltz, *raison d'etat* and *realpolitik* do not only describe; they are part of an explanation of what will always be the case.

This is not quite prescription since prescription is beside the point in a deterministic system.   Nevertheless the interpretation of political reality implicitly given has many normative implications. The view of international relations as necessarily a power game ruled by *realpolitik* undermines any attempt to bring other values to bear on interstate transactions. The perception of *realpolitik* as a common form of behavior or a major pressure (temptation) is quite different from Waltz's structural determinism.

If behavior governed by *realpolitik* is considered necessary for survival then the conditions which cause the security dilemma can only increase. It used to be possible to achieve security through military strength or military alliances. If security broke down the worst that could happen was a war. Today security cannot be bought and we cannot afford a major war.

Morality in public policy is not a matter of all or nothing.

Any policy is animated by some kind of morality. *Realpolitik* narrows the focus of morality to the power interests of one's own state.   Theoretically *realpolitik* would encourage cooperation where parochial and universal interests overlap. However, *realpolitik* undermines conditions of cooperation such as mutual trust.

The arms race is an example of this.   It is not hard to demonstrate that both sides would greatly benefit from an equal reduction in weaponry.   However, with the assumption that both sides will cheat in any way they can, neither dares risk the possibility that the other will secretly exploit arms reduction to improve its position.   If competition is unrestrained, even minimal trust is not needed. The major barrier to the success of current arms negotiations is not national interest but lack of trust. *Realpolitik* is not just a result of the security dilemma; it is a cause of the security dilemma as well.

Nuclear Weapons and the Meaning of Power

The key term in realist theory is power.   In Waltz's structural theory the struggle for power is a necessary result of the anarchic system.   It cannot be denied that there are structures of relationship in international politics in which power plays an important role.   But how those structures are interpreted and what power means in them cannot be objectively determined because the perspective of the analyst deeply influences interpretation.

There is no such thing as an objectively existing world system or order that can be defined irrespective of one's perspective.   For example the phrase, "A is more powerful than B," depends on a selective interpretation of the meaning of power. The same phenomenon may be read, "A is oppressing B", or even "A needs B."   The values that are attached to the term power must be interpreted from a particular standpoint.

In 1959 John Herz penned the famous line that "absolute power equals absolute impotence."[28] On an abstract level this is a self- evident statement. The power to destroy the world cannot be literally used for "lesser" ends. However the simple conclusion drawn that military power has become obsolete in a nuclear age does not follow. As Waltz points out, the usefulness of power should not be equated with its usability.[29] Nonetheless, some of the traditional uses of military power have been inhibited by the advent of nuclear weapons. All military conflict is of grave danger to the security of the most powerful countries because escalation from minor to major warfare can never be ruled out.

Before the nuclear age there was a far more direct connection between military power and the effective ability to coerce a lesser power. A state could go to war if the sovereign did not believe its "just" demands had been respected. This "usability" of military power meant that it often did not need to be used. The threat of war by a greater power was very persuasive.

Stanley Hoffmann says,

> Today...this once fairly persistent link between military strength and positive achievements has been loosened. The power to coerce has never been so great or so evenly distributed...but its nature is now such that its possessor must restrict its uses. The fullest use of nuclear power is in denial, but this must consist in threats—in deterrence—and by definition shuns execution.[30]

Thomas Schelling demonstrated that the power to hurt is no longer contingent upon the ability to defeat. The power to inflict pain should be a very effective means of compellence. However, with nuclear weapons this overwhelming coercive power is restrained by fear. It is dangerous and difficult to make persuasive coercive threats with a power such as nuclear weapons. The danger of nuclear war saps the effectiveness of lesser military threats. Compellance is a psychological process in which there is no easy proportionality between military power and political effectiveness.

Military power is only one of many inputs into the process of political bargaining. In time of extreme crisis it may become the dominant input. Hoffmann says,

Obviously when its survival is at stake, a state will tend
to behave as states have customarily behaved—by
resorting to all-out force. But the novelty lies precisely in
the fact that the great powers try not to challenge too
rudely each other's survival, nor to let others provoke such
a challenge.[31]

This statement needs further qualification. The greatest
threat to the survival of a state is precisely the resort to
all-out war. The *ultima* ratio has not been done away with.
But it has become more deadly than ever before because even
"victory" does not guarantee survival.

In the process of bargaining there are many different kinds
of power; military, economic, political, moral, social,
spiritual, etc. None of these kinds of power can control the
outcome of bargaining between states. Military vulnerability
has a significance that may outweigh other areas of
vulnerability in extreme situations. The outcome of bargaining
in many situations is dependent on an extremely complex web
of circumstances and relations in which military security may
or may not be significant. The cost of a military means to a
political end has always been high. Fighting wars has
always been difficult and costly. However, never before have
the risks and costs of military solutions been so high.

Hoffmann suggests that,

Today, since nations can only make limited use of their
power to punish, they are led to more often use the milder
forms of coercion, the power to reward and the power to
influence—all those forms of power that are not
proportional, and are often unrelated to power as material
supply.[32]

This does not mean that the "great powers" are impotent.
The Soviet Union and the United States are great powers
precisely because they wield many different kinds of power.

Power is not a commodity that can be weighed. The
material aspects of power are not the only, or necessarily the
most significant factors that influence the outcome of political
bargaining.[33] For example, the commitment of a state to a
particular goal may greatly enhance a materially weak

state's position. A politically unified state has an advantage over a divided nation, whatever their proportionate power. A state that can rally international sympathy and support, gains an intangible kind of power. Perhaps the most dramatic kind of non-material power is the willingness to suffer, rather than give in. Persistence and endurance, change the meaning of "vulnerability."

Vietnam's willingness to call Nixon's bluff on the use of nuclear weapons neutralized the huge disproportion in material power between the two countries. Similarly, the taking of American hostages in Iran or Lebanon illustrates the relativity of military power. While Iranian militants held only a few American hostages, in a sense the U.S. nuclear arsenal held hostage the entire country of Iran. Yet it was not U.S. military power which ultimately freed the U.S. hostages. Economic and other pressures proved the more effective.

Stanley Hoffmann argues that,

> ... a study of power in international relations that equates power with coercion and deals with coercion in terms of traditional supply is obsolete. The new and changed restraints on the military dimension of power have led to an emancipation and multiplication of other kinds of power and should lead to a much more diversified (and much less assured) analysis.[34]

Political scientists continually use the word power with a wider reference than armed forces. Whether the focus is on military, political, economic, social, psychological or even spiritual power, the term is a relative one. Power is relational. One is powerful in relation to someone or something else. Power may be internal and potential or it may be expressed.

There are two general categories of power: power to be something and power to do something. The first of these is seldom the topic of international relations theory; nevertheless, it is very relevant to international politics. The "national interest" can be used to indicate the values central to the identity of a nation. The fact that "national interest" is predominantly used to refer to the interest in security, wealth and influence may simply reflect the dominant values of our own culture. The power to be something is more interior than security, wealth and importance. It has to do with the character of a people and the organization of their society.

National character is not separable from the way a nation views power and security. What a state does affects what it becomes. A nation's view of power will be dramatically reflected in how it organizes its resources. When military strength becomes the measure of power and security all other values are subordinated. An overemphasis on military security can have a profound impact on the internal social organization of a nation.[35] Quite apart from the unanswerable question of whether armaments enhance or detract from the possibility of nuclear war, a nation's definition of power influences what it becomes.

Kenneth Waltz defines power as the ability to affect other countries more than they affect you. This assumes that being affected or influenced by another country is a sign of relative powerlessness. Yet the power to be something or achieve something may require less independence and more interdependence or even dependence. Waltz assumes that power is the same as relative independence. Until a few years ago one of the most independent countries in the world was the Peoples Republic of China. The opening of China greatly increased its dependence on the rest of the world. That does not necessarily signify that China is now weaker, only that Chinese leaders have changed their definition of power.

How does one define a balance of power when power has so many different meanings? It cannot be done. A rough "balance" or equity of military forces may be calculated but the relation between military strength and security cannot be calculated. Whether the United States is more secure than Finland is a matter of definition.

Political realism is mistaken in its claim to be an objective explanation of political   reality.   Realism's uncritical assumption of the value and utility of military power leads to a sophisticated naivety about nuclear weapons. If military power is considered the ruling factor in international politics then nuclear weapons may be considered good.

A Structural Realists View of Nuclear Weapons

Kenneth Waltz has written a stark and lucid contradiction of the rising anti-nuclear sentiment that is partially reflected in this book.[36] He says that because nuclear weapons have rendered major warfare extremely undesirable for all involved, we should welcome nuclear weapons as a great influence for peace. The spread of nuclear weapons is not to be feared but rather welcomed as a potent dampener of war. In short, the more nations that have nuclear weapons, the better, because with nuclear weapons many of the factors that caused war in the past are removed.

The link between Waltz's argument and structural theory is important. Waltz uses structural language to add strength or certainty to his conclusions. This is important because his conclusions lose their appeal if they are uncertain. It is difficult to welcome the spread of nuclear weapons if there is any chance that they will be used.

The major structural aspect of Waltz's perception of nuclear weapons is that the international structure is bipolar and hence dominated and policed by two invulnerable powers. Neither great power can use nuclear weapons because of mutual deterrence. And neither power will allow anyone else in the world to use nuclear weapons. In contrast to the confusion and intrigue of a multipolar world, a bipolar world is characterized by, "self-dependence of parties, clarity of dangers (and) certainty about who has to face them."[37]

Waltz's ruling assumption is that war is the result of each nation rationally following its self-interest in a state of nature. If it is clear that war involving nuclear powers is against everyone's self-interest then no war will occur except by miscalculation. Miscalculation is practically impossible in a conflict involving a nuclear superpower. Because the disaster of a nuclear war is indisputable,

> ... the presence of nuclear weapons makes states exceedingly cautious. Think of Kennedy and Khrushchev in the Cuban missile crisis. Why fight if you can't win much and might lose everything?[38]

For Waltz the peaceful outcome of the Cuban missile crisis was a necessary outcome of rational actors faced with the potential results of a nuclear war. However, an opposite interpretation of those same events is possible. If both parties were totally rational each could have assumed that the other would back down rather than go to war. Gradual escalation makes it very difficult for either to back down. Khruschev's decision to comply with Kennedy's ultimatum may have led to his political downfall. With different leaders a war might well have occurred.

Waltz recognizes that miscalculation causes wars. But, he says, nuclear weapons reduce the danger of miscalculation to a minimum.

> Countries armed with conventional weapons go to war knowing that even in defeat their suffering will be limited... If countries armed with nuclear weapons go to war they do so knowing that their suffering may be unlimited.[39]

In a battle of nerves, thè same course of action may be considered rational if it induces the opponent to back down, and irrational if it leads to nuclear war. Waltz's overly simple model posits that nuclear war is very unlikely. That assumption is probably incorrect. Unfortunately, rational self-interest is indeterminate in a battle of nerves.

Politicians are not only subject to misperception, but also subject to willful distortion of reality. Distortion of reality is not just a personal phenomenon. States are amazingly complex organisms that are subject to the collective distortions of special interest groups, bureaucratic imperatives, structural rigidities and many types of political pressures.

The distortion of a nation's self-interest is demonstrated by an amazing anomaly in Waltz's own work. According to Waltz's analysis of rational deterrence, the stability of deterrence is unaffected by the arms race. He says,

> That we have ten thousand warheads to the Soviet Union's six thousand makes us no worse and no better off than we were when the ratio was even more favorable. That the throw-weight of the Soviet Union's missiles

exceeds ours by several times makes us no better and no worse off than it would be were the ratio to be reversed.[40]

If this is so then, why in a self-help system, do the great powers spend so much on strategic arms? Waltz's implication that it is because they have the economic power to sustain an even useless arms race is not convincing.

A more likely explanation is that the great powers continue to accept the obsolete realist image of security based on a balance of military power. Classical balance of power theory never envisaged the practically infinite overkill capacity of nuclear weapons. The very theory that Waltz so ably defends leads to measuring security in terms of military balance.

Waltz makes the troubling suggestion that the only rational purpose for an arms race after finite deterrence is reached is to achieve a first strike capability. While he discounts first strike as a possible motivation "because of its irrationality," the only remaining possibility is that other, equally irrational forces prompt the arms race. Waltz said,

> With deterrent strategies arms races make sense only if a first strike capability is within reach. Because thwarting a first strike is easy, deterrent forces are quite cheap to build and maintain.[41]

Waltz's faith in the rational pressures of a self-help system are further displayed in his attitude to the use of tactical nuclear weapons. Waltz ignores the symbolic value of the nuclear firebreak and suggests that if strategic deterrence can prevent large wars, then an emphasis on the battlefield use of tactical nuclear weapons should prevent small wars as well. His reason is that battle field use of small nuclear weapons would make defense impregnable and aggression useless. Early use of tactical nuclears would prevent conventional escalation by making it clear to the aggressor that the war cannot be won without resort to strategic weapons.

There are many problems with this prescription. The central one is that Waltz persists in overestimating the rational ability of political leaders to control events. The difficulties of de-escalation in a war between superpowers is immense. Even if tactical weapons were carefully used on the battlefield, there is no clear limit for weapons size or norms for permissible collateral damage. The line between tactical and strategic weapons is not clear and even counterforce tactical use could be mistaken for strategic use in highly populated areas such as Europe. Waltz makes the potentially fatal assumption that aggressors will be rational and retreat from confrontation if tactical nuclear weapons are used against them. What if an opponent operates by the same logic and does not retreat?

In discussing the use of nuclear weapons by lesser powers, Waltz suggests that they would only do so if their survival was at stake. "And this should be called not irresponsible but responsible use."[42] If political survival is at stake, even nuclear war is permissible to save the state.

Waltz denies that the use of nuclear weapons by a lesser power would pull in the superpowers or initiate major war. On this point he is inconsistent. One of the reasons Waltz gives for the unlikelihood of nuclear blackmail by a lesser power is the danger of retaliation from other nuclear powers. Yet Waltz affirms the converse at another point,

And the use of nuclear weapons by lesser powers would hardly trigger them elsewhere, with the U.S. and the U.S.S.R. becoming involved in ways that might shake the central balance.[43]

The problem is that it is impossible to say what course nuclear (or even conventional) conflict would take. In complex situations it is easy to select different factors at different times to support our own predilection. When dangers are deterred with dangers it is impossible to determine with absolute certainty how real events will turn out. Waltz does not expect small nuclear powers ever to have to use nuclear weapons precisely because in a crisis they would have to use them. Their weakness in non-nuclear defense provides a powerful deterrent to any would-be aggressor because they would have to meet aggression with nuclear weapons. Waltz focuses on the security of deterrence based on great danger.

Waltz's optimism about the future stability of deterrence is partly based on the relative peace the world has enjoyed since the advent of nuclear weapons. He suggests that it is odd that a happy nuclear past leads many to expect an unhappy nuclear future. There are two problems with nuclear optimism based on the past. The first is that forty years is not very long in relation to the danger. There only needs to be one major nuclear war to end industrial civilization. We have come close enough to nuclear war to cause definite uneasiness about living for the indefinite future with the same threat.

Waltz's reasoning is similar to that of nuclear energy proponents who point out that no one was killed at Three Mile Island. None or few have died yet from that disaster, but the state of Pennsylvania was almost made uninhabitable. A perfect record is not necessarily reassuring if only one error ends the ball game. Of course we may hope and expect that one "small" nuclear conflict would not lead to the destruction of civilization. But even a small possibility is not comforting.

A second problem with optimism based on the past is counting probabilities. Probabilities have no concrete meaning in relation to unprecedented events. However, if we arbitrarily assign a one percent chance of nuclear war, the outlook in any given year is very good. The overall odds for fifty years is only fifty percent and the really long term prospects are very grim. Nevertheless the condition is quite likely to persist because there is never an urgent need to solve the problem. Each individual year discloses very little danger. With this perspective in mind, Waltz's arguments for the unlikelihood of nuclear war may be correct without offering the reassurance he intends.

One reason a radical attempt to reduce the number of nuclear weapons is unlikely to be welcomed by political leaders is that any major disturbance in the settled habits of states may increase the short term probability of nuclear war. Thus the long term route to disaster is structurally reinforced by "rational actors in a self-help system."

It should be clarified that Waltz does not advocate a costly strategic arms race that focuses on war-fighting rather than deterrence. While he does not appear particularly troubled by the strategic arms race, Waltz does not believe it is necessary for the purposes of deterrence. The starting point for Waltz, as for all realists, is with politically viable alternatives, given the actual state of the world. Waltz is not concerned with ideal policy.

> Fearing the world's destruction, one may prefer a world of conventional great powers having a higher probability of fighting less destructive wars to a world of nuclear great powers having a lower probability of fighting more destructive wars. But that choice effectively disappeared with the production of atoms bombs by the U.S. during World War II.[44]

If nuclear weapons are here to stay then there is not much point, according to Waltz, of bemoaning their danger. Waltz concludes that, "the gradual spread of nuclear weapons is better than no spread and better than rapid spread."[45] If the basic equilibrium of the balance of power system is maintained then the pressures of a self-help structure will prevent war. The more costly war becomes the less likely it becomes. Nuclear weapons raise the costs and lower the likelihood. Therefore more nuclear weapons are better than less.

Structural realism assumes that the invisible hand of the self- help system will prevent irrational war. According to Waltz, world leaders need not even be rational to ensure that nuclear weapons will not be used. Such reasoning should have prevented all the costly wasteful wars of the twentieth century. Waltz says it did not because of misperception in the complexity of a multipolar world. Unfortunately, invisible hands have a tendency to disappear when they are most needed. Waltz has pointed out that nuclear weapons produce many pressures that lessen the likelihood of war. That is true, but it misses the point that they also acutely threaten the continued viability of human existence.

Conclusion

The metaphors and symbols of realism are still the dominant *themata* in international relations theory, in spite of weaknesses in the assumptions from which their concepts are deduced.

One explanation is that the concepts of balance of power, state of nature, *realpolitik*, national interest, *raison d'etat* and the security dilemma are powerful symbols which communicate on an emotional level vague ideas that are universally understood. Another reason is that those concepts are elusive: their meaning changes to fit different situations. Thirdly, realist metaphors cannot be disproved if stated carefully. Moreover there are numerous historical situations which seem to empirically fit realist theory.

But perhaps the major support of realist theory is the lack of a viable alternative. International relations theory lacks an overarching theory that can replace the metaphors of realism. Perhaps the closest attempt at an ideal type is the "complex interdependence" of Keohane and Nye. But many theorists find it more fruitful to struggle for "bits" of theory in limited areas of international relations rather than continue a stale battle over abstract concepts.

A realist world view is to a certain extent a self-fulfilling prophecy. The key is to find an alternative symbol system that will rival the power of realism in forming people's perception of the world. For Christians, a world view is linked to an understanding of God's work in history. An urgent, prophetic task for the Church is to link a theological understanding of international politics to an accurate perception of the forces at work in international relations.

Realism challenges Christians to address ethical questions to actual human behavior and resist the temptation to pose political solutions that are impossible.

Realism also challenges ethics to recognize the structured pressures of the international system. Ethical criticism too often assumes that political behavior is simply a matter of will, or of choices between good and evil. Ethical, political criticism must find and highlight other pressures which can rival the antagonistic thrust of a self-help system.

On a political level, the ethical task is to mitigate the pressures of survival that squeeze out the possibility of ethical freedom. In the case of nuclear weapons, the task is to encourage the perception that survival is not enhanced by military competition.

Ethical inquiry into nuclear politics must confront realism with insight into the present effects of nuclear weapons on the character of a nation as well as on the future of the world. If the pressures of a self-help system are accepted as part of the picture, the question is, how can they be mitigated? We may ideally ask what ought to be the dominant pressure on a "good" nation. But the question will only be useful if it is coupled with increased political pressures that pull in a positive direction. The definition of politically plausible positive directions is a key problem. But international relations urgently needs to decrease the fatal reliance on nuclear weapons.

In our final chapter, we discuss why Christians must work within the political constraints of government for realistic alternatives to a nuclear defense policy. However, we will also discuss how the imperatives of faith require Christians to step outside the logic of political causation and engage in a politics of witness and protest.

1   Werner Levi, "The Relative Irrelevance of Moral Norms in International Relations," in James N. Rosenthau ed., *International Politics and Foreign Policy: A Reader in Research and Theory* (New York: Free Press, 1961), pp. 191ff. The popularity of this perception is made particularly vivid to me by the shocked or blank expressions on the faces of people who hear I work in ethics and international relations. A common response is "What? I didn't know they had anything to do with each other!"

2   Kenneth W. Thompson in "The Nuclear Dilemma—A Discussion," *Christianity and Crisis*, XXI, No. 19 (November 13, 1961): 200-204.

3   Niccolo Machiavelli, *The Prince*, W.K. Marriot, trans., *The Great Books* vol. 23 (Chicago: *Encyclopaedia Britannica*, 1952).

4   Thomas Hobbes, *Leviathan*, Nelle Fuller, ed., *The Great Books*, Vol. 23 (Chicago: *Encyclopaedia Britannica*, 1952), ch. XIII, p. 85.

5   Ibid., p. 86.

6   Ibid., p. 86.

7   Rousseau's exposition of the origin of the social contract in The Origin of Inequality contradicted the description he gave for it in his more mature work, *The Social Contract*. The difference may be accounted for partly by Rousseau's "mellowing" of views about civilization and partly by the fact that the later contract is an ideal type, while the earlier contract is the result of his speculative attempt to reconstruct history. See Jean-Jacques Rousseau, *The Origin of Inequality*, in *The Great Books*, vol. 83 (Chicago: Encyclopaedia Britannica, 1952), p. 351. Cf. *The Social Contract*, ibid., p. 397.

8   Jean-Jacques Rousseau, *A Lasting Peace through the Federation of Europe and the State of War*, C.E. Vaughan, trans. (London: Constable, 1917), pp. 59-60.

9   See G.W.F. Hegel, *Philosophy of Right* (Oxford: Clarendon Press, 1942), p. 264. Cf. Friedrich Meinecke, *Machiavellism* (New Haven, Conn.: Yale University Press, 1957), p. 8.

10   Cf. Thucydides, *The Peleponnesian War*, trans., Rex Warner (Harmondsworth: Penguin Books, 1954) and Kautilya, Arthasastra. See George Modelski "Kautilya: Foreign Policy and International System in the Ancient Hindu World." *American Political Science Review*, LVIII (September, 1964): 549-560.

11   David Hume, *Essays and Treatises on Several Subject* (Edinburgh: Bell and Bradfute and W. Blackwood, 1825), I, pp. 331- 339. Reprinted in Arned Lijphart, ed. (Boston: Allyn and Bacon, 1966), pp. 228-234.

12 James E. Dougherty and Robert L. Pflatzgraff, *Contending Theories of International Relations* (New York: J.B. Lippincott, 1971), p. 7. E.H. Carr defined the utopians as those whose attitude was, "if it won'twork it must be made to work." Cf. Edward Hallett Carr, *The Twenty Years Crisis, 1919-1939: An Introduction to the Study of International Relations* (New York: Harper and Row, 1964), p. 8.

13 Ibid., p. 62.

14 Kenneth N. Waltz, *Theory of International Relations* (Menlo Park, CA: Addison-Wesley, 1979).

15 Ibid., p. 118.

16 Ibid., p. 121.

17 Ibid., p. 121.

18 I am particularly indebted to Ernst B. Haas for some of these ideas about what he terms "formal, deductive, deterministic systems theory."

19 See Hans Morgenthau, *Politics Among the Nations*, 4th ed. (New York: Alfred A. Knopf, 1967), pp. 161-166.

20 Ernst B. Haas, "The Balance of Power: Prescription, Concept or Propaganda?" *World Politics* V (July, 1953): 442-447.

21 S.F. Nadel, *The Theory of Social Structure* (Glencoe, IL: Free Press, 1957), p. 148.

22 Ibid., p. 141ff.

23 Robert Keohane and Joseph Nye, *Power and Interdependence* (New York: Little, Brown and Co., 1977). See especially chapter two for a contrast of the assumptions of realism and complex interdependence.

24 Quoted in Ibid., p. 26.

25 Quoted in Donella H. Meadows, et al., *The Limits to Growth* (New York: Signet, 1972), p. 21.

26 Stanley Hoffmann, *Duties Beyond Borders* (New York: Syracuse University Press, 1981), p. 17.

27 Waltz, *Theory of International Politics*, p. 117.

28 John H. Herz, *International Politics in the Atomic Age* (New York: Columbia University Press, 1959), pp. 22, 169.

29 Waltz, *Theory of International Politics*, p. 185.

30 Stanley, Hoffmann, *Gulliver's Troubles or the Setting of American Foreign Policy* (New York: McGraw-Hill, 1968), p. 29.

31 Ibid., p. 31.

32 Ibid., p. 30.

33 See Keohane and Nye, p. 17f.

34 Hoffmann, *Gulliver's Troubles*, p. 32.

35 See Harold D. Lasswell, "The Garrison State Hypothesis Today", in Samuel P. Huntington, ed., *Changing Patterns of Military Politics* (New York: The Free Press of Glencoe, 1962). See my discussion of these issues in chapter one.

36 Kenneth N. Waltz, *The Spread of Nuclear Weapons: More May be Better*, Adelphi Paper No. 171 (London: The International Institute for Strategic Studies, Autumn, 1981).

37 Ibid., p. 3.

38 Ibid., p. 5.

39 Ibid., p. 6.

40 Ibid., p. 15. See Robert Jervis, "Why Nuclear Superiority Doesn'tMatter," *Political Science Quarterly*, Vol, 94 (Winter 1979-1980).

41 Waltz, More May be Better, p. 22.

42 Ibid., p. 19.

43 Ibid., p. 13.

44 Ibid., p. 24.

45 Ibid., p. 28.

CHAPTER VI

THE ACUTE TENSION BETWEEN MORALITY AND NUCLEAR POLICY

In this book I have argued that the nature of war has changed and that the way in which we think about war must change as well.

Since World War II there has not been a single successful attempt to formulate a convincing political morality that could link military strategy to modern technological realities. The best books on morality and international relations do a fine job of criticizing other attempts and opening up the problems of international politics, but they do not provide any master theory. The reason for this failure is quite simple: there is no solution to the problem of ethics and international relations.

The agonizing approach of Augustine of Hippo is still instructive for today's problems. He grasped the tension between freedom and necessity, between justice and love and between Christian morality and practical politics. Augustine's solution of internalizing love was inadequate. But the tension he displayed illuminated the problem. Nuclear weapons have highlighted and intensified this tension as never before.

Christians must recognize that there is a flat contradiction between the apparent political requirements of nuclear policy and Christian ethics. This contradiction cannot be resolved by isolating nuclear policy from intent in the manner of J. Bryan Hehir or by refusing to verbalize the threat as Francis Winter suggests. Even the assertion of a "supreme emergency" by Michael Walzer does no more than imply that ethics are no longer relevant to the extremity of nuclear necessity. Waltz's claim that nuclear weapons will usher in a world without major war is, to use Stanley Hoffmann's term, "panglossian."[1] It also denies the relevance of the ethical question.

In this chapter I reformulate the old question of how Christian ethical ideals can be relevant to international politics and propose ways to creatively work with the tension between conscience and policy. Differences of perspective, possibility and responsibility lead to two different approaches to the possibility of nuclear war.

The ethics of Christian discipleship are in absolute contradiction to many values that animate the arms race. At the same time, Christian ideals must address the realities of practical politics. Christian policy makers can relate the ideal to political realities only if they carefully distinguish between actual policy, possible policy, realistic policy, desirable policy and Christian abstract ideals.

Most Christians are not policy makers. My conclusions address the responsibility they bear for the nuclear world in which they live.

Reframing the Question

The questions asked by just war theory and political realism fail to address the issues of modern war. Throughout much of its history just war theory started with the question, how may wars be fought justly? A question of realism was, how can the balancing of power produce security? We must ask new questions. What Stephen Neill said of philosophy is also true of Christian political ethics:

> But each generation comes with its own questions; and more than we perhaps care to realize, the answer is already determined by the nature of the questions that we put. We read Plato and Aquinas and Kant for inspiration and the disciplining of our minds; but their questions are not our questions...[2]

War has always been a terrible reality which men and women have sought to avoid. But never before has war threatened the very survival of the world's ecosystem. The urgency of the problem prompts the questions: How may we live without war? or, How may we abolish nuclear weapons? Jonathan Schell recently asked these questions and arrived at the same answer as the nineteenth century utopians: we must reinvent politics, achieve worldwide disarmament, (both conventional and nuclear), and form a world government.[3] Without detracting from the need to ask those questions and pose radical solutions to them, I would like to suggest a more modest question.

The primary moral political question in international relations today may be: How can we reduce the criminal burden of the possession of nuclear weapons? the question "How" indicates that it is not just a moral problem but a technical and political problem as well. To renounce nuclear weapons may be helpful but it does not take us far.

"We" implies that this is a corporate problem. Nuclear weapons are the product of our technological culture. They are not separable from the vast network of scientfic, technological and social structures of life by which, and in which, we live. Responsibility for nuclear weapons lies with all of us, not just with the scientific, political and military elite. At the most superficial level of responsibility, we all pay for nuclear weapons.[4] We elect the leaders who control them.

On the other hand, "criminal" implies that nuclear weapons are not just a technical problem but a moral problem. Nuclear weapons are not morally neutral. They are weapons of genocide. After all of the complex arguments regarding political necessity, deterrence and legitimate defense are finished, it can still be said, "It's wrong to build a nuclear weapon." The moral problem of nuclear weapons remains irrespective of whether they are intended to be used or intended only to prevent the use of other weapons. Even an intensely pacifistic motivation behind the production of nuclear weapons could not hide the fact that their existence constitutes an objective, immoral threat and the material means for its execution.

The term "burden" implies that there is a present, ongoing cost to the possession of nuclear weaplons, that outweighs any benefits they may produce. This is a subjective judgement because it is impossible to measure either the costs or the benefits of nuclear weapons. The greatest cost undoubtedly lies in the future, if and when they are used in warfare. Their present cost is also considerable. World arms expenditures are presently at about $550 billion a year, which amounts to a million dollars every minute. It has been estimated that ten hours of such spending could go far to eliminate the entire world's hunger problem.[5]

The costs of nuclear weaponry include many non-economic costs that cannot be measured and that may be hardly felt. In 1960, Eric Fromm wrote,

> To live for any length of time under the constant threat of destruction creates certain psychological effects in human beings—fright, hostility, callousness—and a resulting indifference to all the values we cherish. Such conditions will transform us into barbrians.[6]

Similarly, John Bennett asked, "How can a nation live with its conscience and know that it is preparing to kill 20 million children in another nation if the worst should come to the worst."[7]

In contrast, Michael Walzer suggests that the striking fact about deterrence is how easy it is to live with. He says of deterrence,

> The strategy works because it is easy. Indeed it is easy in a double sense; not only don'twe do anything to other people, we also believe that we will never have to do anything...[8]

These differences point out the difficulty of measuring the psychological costs of nuclear weapons. We may safely asssume that conditions would be different without an arms race. Positively speaking, the world would be quite different if even a fraction of the resources, time and expertise devoted to defense were applied to social problems. Social, psychological and spiritual costs cannot be measured but may outweigh the economic costs.[9]

A realization of the costs does not help solve the question of "how" the problem of nuclear weapons may be mitigated, but a perception of the cost of the arms race can clarify the nature of the "burden" which nuclear weaponry constitutes. Massive demonstrations in Europe and the continuing public outcry against nuclear weapons in the United States indicates that the burden of nuclear weapons is being felt at the grassroots level.

The way in which a question is stated defines the questioner's relation to the problem. The quesiton, "How can we reduce the criminal burden of the possession of nuclear weapons?", contains in it the pessimintic assumption that nuclear weapons cannot be abolished in the foreseeable future. The question assumes that there is no solution to the problem. However, the burden of the problem and the problem itself may be reduced.

Tensions in a Political Approach to the Nuclear Problem

The simplest formulation of the political problem of nuclear weapons is that they are both intolerable and permanent. They are intolerable because there is a possibility of their destroying most of the world. They are permanent for two reasons. First, unless industrial society is destroyed there will always be people who know how to make nuclear weapons. Even if total disarmament were achieved, nuclear weapons could be rapidly manufactured by an advanced industrial society in the event of war. Nuclear weapons will always be a threat. Secondly, the political possibilities of complete nuclear disarmament are so slim as to be negligible. Arms reduction is a possibility worth working for. Complete disarmament is impossible in a world of distrust and conflict. Rational suspicion and self-protection are unlikely to disappear.

The "security dilemma" is not the ruling factor in international relations. It is descriptive of a part of reality. Both the structure of international relations and what Christians call "fallen human nature" provide an enduring basis for reasonable insecurity. Nuclear weapons are not hard to hide or break down into components. Even if disarmament were agreed upon there would be no way to stop cheating.

The political necessity of nuclear weapons is in one sense merely a matter of the polls. If enough people could be persuaded to change their mind and support disarmament then it would be possible. If it happened in Holland, why not here? There are many reasons why not. One is fear of the Soviet

Union. Holland's nuclear weapons are insignificant in relation to deterrence. Those of the United States are essential. Roger Shinn articulates an undeniable fear. While he supports dramatic unilateral initiatives, he rejects major unilateral disarmament. He says,

> It would not enhance the peace of the world. The one situation more dangerous and more fraught with injustice than a balance of terror is a monopoly of terror. The unilateral renunciation of nuclear weapons may be a rational and ethically responsible act for some nations. It is not a political possibility for all nations.[10]

Fear of the Soviet Union is not just a psychological condition that may be replaced with trust by an act of the will. The Soviet Union might very well increase aggressive and oppressive activity all over the world if it were unimpeded by nuclear deterrence. Of course, the U.S. will not disarm for many reasons besides fear. These include technological and bureaucratic momentum, the international influence and prestige of being a superpower, both internal and foreign economic interests and ideological opposition to communism.

The immorality and political necessity of nuclear weapons cannot be reconciled within a single political strategy. Part of the problem has to do with the necessity of the use of power in political relations. Reinhold Niebuhr wrestled cogently with this issue. The need for justice in the relationship between groups requires that each group's power be limited by the power of others. Unimpeded power is dangerous. Waltz argues that it is also impossible. Nation states will do all they can to prevent their rivals from gaining an unqualified advantage over them. For Niebuhr this was an ethical issue. Unimpeded power would lead to great injustice in the world. No nation is virtuous enough to be trusted with an unopposed ability to work its will on the world. The inescapable conclusion of this line of reasoning is that if one nation has nuclear weapons, justice and/or necessity requires that at least one other nation also have them.

In conflict with this line of thought is the stark truth that the evils restrained by nuclear deterrence are far outweighed by the evils of nuclear war. It has always been questionable whether the issues over which wars are fought outweigh the destructiveness of war. In the past it was at least plausible to argue that they did. It is no longer plausible. If the destructiveness of conventional warfare could be seen as preventing an even greater evil, the same could never be said for nuclear war. The evil it threatens cannot be surpassed.

According to Anatol Rapoport, the result is an absolute opposition between strategy and conscience. They cannot both be brought into focus because each assumes a different view of the world. The core of this difference lies in their evaluation of power. Strategy elevates power to the highest level of value. Conscience considers the consequences of power. Rapoport's proposed solution is to convert the strategy thinkers into conscience thinkers by changing their image of the Russians. If fewer people cared about power there would be less conflict. While this is undoubtedly true, it begs the question of how power can be restrained in the real world. Rapoport's description of the tension between conscience and strategy is cogent. But in pointing out the moral and rational bankruptcy of pure strategy he has fallen into the trap of reducing the whole problem to one of conscience. Aggressive power cannot be simply restrained by conscience. Strategists frequently commit the opposite error of reducing the whole problem to technique.

The root of the contradiction between strategy and conscience is much stronger than either the will to peace or the techniques of security through power. The problems that conscience perceives cannot be eliminated by changed attitudes and perspectives. The great realist classics have shown that there are structural insecurities in international relations that foster conflict. Yet beyond the problems of structure there is the reality of evil.

Christians believe that human beings are not simply the pawns of their environment. The root of international conflict cannot be explained by that antispectic concept, "rational self-interest." Rational self-interest begs the question of what it is rational for the self to be interested in! Christians believe that the fundamental cause of the conflict lies in the rejection of God. Human beings place the central value of their lives on themselves. Instead of worshipping God, we worship ourselves.   The root cause of conflict is human self-centeredness. The lack of peace ultimately lies in the human heart. Augustine said,

> On our earthly pilgrimage we pant after peace, yet are involved in constant strife—with the pagan, with the heretic, with the bad Catholic, and even with the brother in the same household. One may grow weary and exclaim, 'Why should I eat out my life in contention? I will return within myself.' Yet even there one will find that the flesh lusts against the spirit.[11]

Augustine saw the lack of worship of God as the root of all evil. Love of God and neighbor cannot be separated, so this rejection of God is played out through domination of others. "It is thus that pride in its perversity apes God. It abhors equality with other men under Him; but instead of His rule it seeks to impose a rule of its own upon equals."[12]

A Christian account of the problem of nuclear weapons must take seriously the problem of evil. Nuclear weapons represent the pinnacle of the human search for god-like power over the environment and each other. Nuclear weapons are a metaphor of the amazing potential for good and evil that animates human beings. Whether or not one assumes a determinative human "nature" to account for it, the results of evil can be objectively observed in personal, societal and international conflict.

Perspective, Possibility and Responsibility in Political Ethics

Three major factors require a difference between the ethics of conscience and the ethics of policy. These factors are perspective, possibility and responsibility.

Perspective

Citizens and policy makers perceive different aspects of political problems. A policy maker may or may not see more than the citizen. Each has a different perspective on the problem and is in touch with different kinds of facts.[13] The questions and problems that frame each person's perception of an issue are different. Politicians should have more information that relates to policy making just as the technical community has more information on the relative efficiency of weapons systems. Either may be blind to aspects of the problem perceived by an informed citizen.

Different perspectives do not necessarily imply a separation between ethic for citizens and an ethic for politicians. Informed citizens are capable of perceiving the perspective of a policy maker and policy makers are also citizens. But when the inescapable and imperative ethical conclusions of the citizen cannot fit within the boundaries of current political possibility strong moral tension is inescapable.

The tension is not between public and private life. Both the policy maker and the citizen are concerned with the same social issues. But the way each perceives the issues and responds to them may be different. Neither has an "absolute" perspective on how an issue should be resolved. But the citizen is not as circumscribed in his or her response by the necessities of policy formation.

Possibility

The logic of political causation places barriers around the limits of political possibility. These barriers may not be as absolute as they seem. Many of the most significant social movements in history ignored the conventional logic of the politically possible. For example, the anti-slavery movement destroyed structures that were presumed immutable. Many logically strong arguments were made for the structural necessity of slavery, yet they could not stand before a strong movement of people who denied historical determinism. The primary momentum for the abolitionist movement did not initially come from the efforts of those who worked within the policy process but from those who opposed "necessity."

The borders of political possibility are real. Movements that change the definition of the possible are also real but they too follow the logic of political causation, albeit in unexpected ways. Political idealism is often important because it ignores the logic of political causation altogether. The imperative of a personal, ethical response to nuclear weapons must be matched by a political ethic that works within (or against) the boundaries of political causation and accepts the different ethical constraints imposed by those boundaries.

Responsibility

A third factor in the contrast between conscience and policy ethics is that of responsibility. Politicians have a responsibility to a large and pluralistic constituency. They are also responsible to work within the borders of political possibility. To advocate programs or policies that have no chance of success is either foolishness, propaganda or symbolic protest. Only the latter can have any moral value. A politician who refuses to support any program that has morally questionable elements in it will accomplish very little. Politics is a method, to use Niebuhr's words, "of finding proximate solutions for insolvable problems."[14]

Christian individuals and communities have a different responsibility in relation to insolvable political problems. They are often ignorant of the necessities of concrete decision-making. Like the politician they are responsible first of all to their conscience. But unlike the politician they are not required to know the complex contingencies of specific policy choices. On the basis of conscience a citizen may repudiate national policy and refuse to abide by it. He or she may work for a change in the perceived national interest of the country and may place transnational values above the national interest. The citizen may reject all of the options among which the policy maker must choose and press for a redefinition of the problem. Most significantly, the citizen can deny the supremacy of governmental actors and address political problems through other agencies. For the individual, governmental policy may not be the most significant factor in the solution to a political problem.

Two Linked but Separate Approaches to Christian Political Ethics

Dualistic approaches are common in this history of Christian political ethics. Augustine's contrast between the city of God and the city of "man", Luther's two kingdoms, the Anabaptist contrast between Kingdom ethics and worldly ethics and Niebuhr's dualism of individual and corporate ethics are all attempts to deal with the tension we have outlined.[15]

Most approaches tended to over-emphasize one side of the duality they propose. Thus Anabaptist ethics emphasized separation from political compromise and strict allegiance to Kingdom ethics. Niebuhr emphasized the impossibility of purity and the need to take moral risks for the sake of political justice. Luther held the two in tension but allowed far too sharp a separation between personal and public responsibility. The result was too great a separation between personal morality and political problems.

Augustine attempted a resolution through spiritualizing the meaning of love and separating intent from action. None of these approaches can adequately address the problems posed by nuclear weapons.

Political Responsibility and Christian Ideals

In different ways, John Howard Yoder and Reinhold Niebuhr have illuminated the problem of political responsibility for Christian ethics. Like Yoder, I assume that non-violence is the norm for the Christian but that, "in our present age it is impossible to do away with the need for violent action in the political or economic realm."[16] Yoder rejects the separation of personal from political ethics. Christian ethics are inescapably political but one cannot require the same standards of behavior from the state as are encumbant upon the Christian. He says,

> We need to distinguish between the ethics of discipleship which are laid upon every Christian believer ... and an ethics of justice within the limits of relative prudence and self-preservation, which is all one can ask of the larger society.[17]

Yoder suggests that the ideals of discipleship revealed in Jesus Christ are indirectly relevant to the state in that relative, middle axioms can be derived from them. These middle axioms call the state to alternative ways of acting that are politically conceivable. They do not define the nature of an ideal state, for that is inconceivable outside of the Kingdom of God. They do suggest ways in which "the state can best fulfill its responsibilities in a fallen society."[18]

Yoder's methodology undercuts the idealism that expects the state to embody non-violent morality. Yoder also refuses to erode the radical political challenge Jesus gave to those who wished to follow him.

An important difference of emphasis between Yoder's approach and my own, concerns Christian participation in government. At least in his earlier writings, Yoder referred to the Christian's relation to the state as primarily that of witness. While he does not categorically deny the legitimacy of Christians holding public office, he does not discuss the tension that results from the same person attempting to follow the absolute call of discipleship and the relative, prudential call of governmental politics at the same time. Yoder assumes that Christians will usually stay out of coercive governmental politics and concentrate their political activity in other areas.

Yoder dethrones the state from its idolatrous pretensions as the greatest source of human good. This is a needed emphasis, especially in a society that hopes for political solutions to all problems. Governmental policy may sometimes be the source of more problems than it solves. Nevertheless, governmental politics is not an area of life that Christians should avoid even though they may refuse some tasks of government.

Most Christians are not called to be politicians. Nor is a political calling higher or more significant than other professions. An honest shoe repairman whose life portrays the values of the Kingdom of God may produce more goodness in the world than an idealistic politican. Nevertheless, governments have a significant influence on the structures of corporate relations in a society. Some Christians are called to political responsibility. In a pluralistic open society Christians share in the corporate responsibility and guilt for the way society is organized.

When Christians take the responsibility of holding public office they will have to act according to the prudential perspectives, possibilities and responsibilities that adhere to their office. This will inevitably result in the tensions of a double calling. Nowhere will this tension be more acute than in the realm of nuclear defense policy.

Teleological Political Ethics

Christian ethics cannot be simply applied to the state. Too often Christians ignore reality and, as William Temple put it, "bleat fatuously of love." Reinhold Niebuhr certainly overemphasized the saintly irrelevance of the life of Jesus in relation to political problems. But the major gap he pointed to between the ideals of love and the necessities of practical politics cannot be denied. As he said, to assert that if only people loved each other all the complex problems of the political order would be solved, begs the most basic problem of human history.[19]

A Christian's individual response to nuclear weapons is not necessarily a gauge of how he or she would formulate policy if put in the pressurized position of a governmental executive. Political policy makers must use strategic, teleogical reasoning. Most decisions are the outcome of a complex, bureaucratic process through which competing interests are compromised. The realist writings of Reinhold Niebuhr, John Herz and others, convincingly suggest that politics involves tragic, moral risk. As Niebuhr commented,

> Political morality must always be morally ambiguous because it cannot merely reject but must also reflect, beguile, harness and use self-interest for the sake of a tolerable harmony of the whole.[20]

Insofar as Christians take part in policy formation they will have to share in the tension, or even anguish of working through a political process in which ethical fervor and moral clarity are sapped by the compromises of necessity. Reinhold Niebuhr drew the extreme conclusion that political ethics are exclusively teleological. He said,

> A political policy cannot be intrinsically evil if it can be approved to be an efficacious instrument for the achievement of a morally approved end. Neither can it be said to be wholly good merely because it seems to make for ultimately good consequences. Immediate consequences must be weighed against the ultimate consequences.[21]

This statement is reasonable in the abstract but impossible in reality. It is not possible to predict all the good and bad consequences of questionable political means. Nowhere is this fact more obvious than in nuclear weapons policy. Teleological ethics over- value human control of history. Policy makers need clear moral and, if possible, legal limits to political behavior.

The problem of indeterminacy in policy areas such as national security requires that deontological principles proscribe the kind of teleological rationalizations that can lead to disaster. An example of a minimum requirement of deontological political morality is the necessity for an unambiguous decision never to use nuclear weapons no matter what the provocation. We will return to this point for further clarification in relation to the requirements of realistic policy. In terms of the broad outlines of policy ethics, Niebuhr's point is well taken. Policy ethics cannot be formulated in terms of abstract ideals. Policy decisions must be made on a relative basis that takes seriously the real possibilities of the political context. In a fallen world, policy ethics must be based on teleological reasoning but circumscribed by deontological limits. Even with such limits, a tension remains between the ethics of policy and the radical imperatives of the teaching of Jesus.

Policy Ethics and Christian Conscience

Luther took the dangerous step of suggesting that Christians may behave differently in public office than in private life. The danger is that if Christians in a public capacity are released from firm principles, they may be open to the infinite rationalizations of political expediency. An extreme example of this danger can be seen in the Lutheran Christians who retained power in the Nazi regime. More recently, former President Jimmy Carter proclaimed with apparent seriousness that if the Soviets launched a nuclear attack, he would promptly launch a nuclear counter-strike.[22] The massive immorality of the threat was apparently neutralized in his mind by the necessities of his office.

A fundamental difference between the tension that inheres in Christian political ethics and classical Lutheran dualism is that I do not believe that a Christian who holds public office is thereby released from the radical imperatives of Christian discipleship.

If an absolute requirement of a governmental position is to carry out immoral, coercive actions, a Christian should resign, even if those actions are considered a necessary lesser evil for the state. A Christian does not cease to be a disciple by virtue of holding political office. A Christian's first allegiance is always to Christ.

A dramatic example of this conviction was shown by Senator Harold Hughs (Dem., Iowa) who withdrew his name from the 1976 presidential campaign on the basis that, as a Christian, he could not threaten the use of nuclear weapons. The implication of this is that a Christian who considered deterrence a politically necessary lesser evil for the nation should not hold any office that was linked to the execution of that policy.

A Christian policy maker must advocate policy based on contingent morality and the least possible evil. Thus, conceivably, a pacifist senator might lobby for a defense policy of "finite deterrence" rather than "flexible options" or "counterforce." If all the available options are considered equally intolerable, a politician is not forced to choose one that is marginally better. All the options may be opposed and other alternatives sought. but policy making demands that choices be made from among real possibilities. As Richard Falk said, "...genuine moral encounter requires that we choose only from among those genuine possibilities implicit within the living tissue of human affairs."[23]

At issue is not whether a Christian can advocate immoral actions and then find someone else to carry them out. If finite deterrence is advocated as a step away from a costly arms race, then someone is already wielding the threat and the power necessary to deterrence. The Christian policy maker is advocating a movement away from a greater to a lesser evil. In abstract terms, finite deterrence or mutually assured destruction is absolutely wrong. However, political morality is not abstract. The person who wields the threat of nuclear deterrence as a real step towards disarmament is part of a process which moves in a direction towards a lesser evil. Innocence or "purity" is not the issue. None of us are innocent. Nevertheless, Christians should avoid participation in "lesser evils" whenever possible.

Christian politicians whose lives are meant to reflect the truth and reality of the Kingdom of God should not carry out or threaten a policy that is in stark contradiction to the Kingdom. Even in political office their personal witness to a reality beyond politics should outweigh political morality. Christians may vote for and advocate a policy that they cannot personally execute because, as the least possible evil available, it is a politically moral policy. Such a policy is ideally the best possible good for the nation at a specific point in time, given the values of the nation and the fallenness of the world.

Refusal to carry out politically necessary policy which appears to be a lesser evil should not be motivated by self-protection. If a Christian condones an interim, nuclear deterrence but personally refuses to issue a deterrent threat, it should not be because of an unwillingness to personally face the Soviet threat without nuclear weapons. This is a tricky area that invites self-deception. Nevertheless, integrity demands that a Christian pacifist be prepared to face the social consequences of non-violence if it were adopted as national strategy. A refusal to carry out a policy of deterrence implies a personal willingness to allow the Soviet Union to have a nuclear monopoly.

In 1947 John Bennett suggested that a policy of non-violence invites suffering on the part of a community which its proponents cannot take upon themselves.[24] In response it can be said that a policy of violence does the same thing, especially if the violence risks the use of nuclear weapons. This whole question may be avoided by acknowledging that a Christian pacifist may support a policy that includes the use of coercion or violence on the basis of relative political reasoning in the direction of a lesser evil. A politician furthermore has a responsibility to his or her constituency, which requires a respect for their values and opinions. Within certain limitations of conscience this may lead the policy maker to support policy he or she does not prefer.

Christian Ideals as a Particular Calling in a Non-Ideal World

Christians should not abstain from morally ambiguous action because they believe such abstention causes them to retain their personal purity. Someone who will not carry a gun is not thereby more pure than a policeman who does. Purity is an elusive quality that may be lost in the very process of seeking it through externals. There is nothing absolutely, inherently wrong in killing a person. In the Old Testament, capital punishment in various situations was law attributed to God.

Christians should be non-violent not because killing is absolutely wrong but because their purpose in life is to reflect and spread the truth revealed in the life of Jesus. Jesus never taught or implied that killing is absolutely wrong. Nor did he imply that suffering without retaliation was an eternal principle of goodness. Rather, he called together a community of disciples who are to display the love and mercy of God through adopting a lifestyle in contrast with the rest of the world. In a world where self-protection and revenge are assumed as rational behavior, they are to break the cycle of "necessity" and reveal the love of God.

The meaning of Christian truth is expressed in action that is related to particular historical situations. This does not imply that there is no truth apart from action but that ethical principles become intelligible only as they are incarnated in specific situations.[25] An implication of this is that Christian ideals that are expressed by a Christian community, may be differently conceived in relation to governments. The reason governments cannot necessarily be expected to "throw themselves on the mercy of God" (Kennan), is that the context of their perspectives, responsibilities and commitments is different from those of the Church.

The meaning of history is not ultimately a different meaning for governments than for the Church. But the ability of each to discern that meaning, and the way in which they can respond to it, will be different. Furthermore the way they should respond to it is different because of their different perspectives, responsibilities and commitments. It is useless to speculate whether or not governmental ethics and Christian ethics would differ in an "unfallen" or "ideal" world. Governmental policy not only cannot but should not be based on Christian ideals in which only a minority believe.

Unlike the Roman Catholic pacifist, Gordon Zahn, I do not believe in the absolute sanctity of life.[26] The reason Christians are to be non-violent has neither to do with realistic political strategies nor with an absolute pacifist principle but with a witness to the love of God, the sovereign reign of Christ and the coming Kingdom.

Non-violence is not simply an optional mode of expressing God's love that the Christian may choose on a contextual basis. It is a *prima facie* requirement of Christian commitment. The teaching, life, death and resurrection of Jesus revealed a style of life that is normative for Christians who seek to follow him. But this normative ethic is based, in part, on the message they bear, (the gospel of peace and reconciliation), their mode of organization, (a church, not a nation-state), and the hope they express, (in the resurrection and the sovereignty of God).

Christian Ideals as a Contradiction to Nuclear Realism

Insofar as Christians relate to political policy questions they must conform their proposals to the logic of political causation. But in their life and witness as individuals and communities they are called to reveal the bankruptcy of the fallen political order by living out a different set of values that break the boundaries of competition and enlightened self-interest. This should not imply blind idealism or hypocritical self-righteousness. The failure of every sector of the Church to live up to Christian ideals is well known. This does not, in itself, invalidate the message. However, it is only where there is a substantial (though imperfect), embodiment of these ideals that they have concrete meaning.

The core of the Gospel is not perfectionism but forgiveness and grace. Christian faith interprets the struggle within individuals and communities as a real moral battle between good and evil. While good and evil are seldom clear cut, the ideals of Christian political behavior are clear.

In governmental politics the primary symbol of power is nuclear weapons. Thermonuclear bombs represent the power to destroy. In the New Testament the primary symbol of power is the cross. The cross represents the power of suffering love. Jesus displayed a power that neither acquiesced to evil nor sought to destroy those who opposed him. At the cross Jesus accepted suffering and returned forgiveness. This was not a "realistic" approach that "succeeded" in preserving his own security or political goals. But Jesus broke the power of the security dilemma by abandoning his own life in allegiance to higher values.

Jesus displayed a power of goodness that profoundly threatened the political authorities of his own day. The power he displayed could not be defeated by military force. He called his disciples to stop worrying about material security, to turn the other cheek when attacked, to give double when robbed, to return good for evil, to forgive when wronged. In short, he wanted them to lose their lives in order to find life.[27] The total life and teaching of Jesus illustrated a radical transformation of political, economic and social values.

John Yoder summarizes the new pattern of values as follows:

> ... a new way to deal with offenders, by forgiving them... a new way to deal with violence—by suffering... a new way to deal with money—by sharing it... a new way to deal with problems of leadership—by drawing upon the gifts of every member, even the most humble... a new way to deal with a corrupt society—by building a new order, not smashing the old... a new pattern of relationships between man and woman, between parent and child, between master and slave in which was made concrete a radical vision of what it means to be a human person.[28]

In governmental politics the means of security for one group constitutes a threat to the security of another. Christians are to break the vicious circle of insecurity in their own relations by placing their security in transcendant values that cannot be destroyed.[29] It is not that physical security is unimportant but rather that there are other values that are more important. True security is only found through trust in God. Jesus says,

> And do not seek what you are to eat and what you are to drink, nor be of anxious mind. For all the nations of the world seek these things; and your Father knows that you need them. Instead, seek his Kingdom and these things shall be yours as well.[30]

Security is not to be found in domination but in servanthood.

You know that those who are supposed to rule over the Gentiles lord it over them...but it shall not be so among you; but whoever would be great among you must be your servant, and whoever would be first among you must be slave of all. For the Son of man also came not to be served but to serve, and to give his life as a ransom for many.[31]

In the Old Testament a frequent theme is the futility of military power as a basis of security. Isaiah, in particular, often contrasts the real security of trust in God with the false security of trust in military alliances. He says,

Woe to those who go down to Egypt for help and rely on horses, who trust in chariots because they are many and in horses because they are very strong, but do not look to the holy one of Israel or consult the Lord.[32]

An Ethic of Conversion

These passages are cited by way of illustration of a theme rather than exegetical proof. Even so it must be admitted that if this does represent an important aspect of Christian political ethics, they are hopelessly "unrealistic." The "politics of Jesus" are not a prescription for the ordering of a just society.

Christians continually fail to live up to this radical vision. Yet many Christians who have been confronted by the claims of Jesus see in his life a call to change the values on which they build their lives. Yoder says,

Jesus will therefore be describing for us a morality of repentance or of conversion; not a prescription of what every man can and should do to be happy; not a meditation on how best to guide a society, but a description of how a person behaves whose life has been transformed by meeting Jesus.[33]

While Christian values cannot be expected to guide the state, they should transform the Christian community's attitude to national values. Over and above the glorification of national prestige and power, a Christian should value the world-wide community of God's people. A Christian's first allegiance is not to the nation-state but to God and to the international Church. Above the nation's quest for economic wealth and prosperity the Church should value biblical justice. The numbing problems of widespread malnutrition and starvation lend an intensified urgency to a Christian opposition to arms spending.

An Ethic of Trust in God

A disciple of Christ must reject the fear, hatred and injustice that characterize the arms race. Christian security is based on a confidence in the sovereignty of God in history not on the ability of nuclear might to deter an attack. The basic command of Jesus to love your enemies rules out threatening them with nuclear devastation, no matter what the provocation.

A transcendent faith does not trivialize or gloss over the terrible evil of nuclear war. It is not permissible to risk the world's destruction because of a belief in meaning beyond history. But faith allows one to say with conviction that it is better to suffer evil than to do it. Jesus did not create the cross. In fact he feared it. But in the end he loved more than he feared.

A dynamic behind the arms race is fear. The same dynamic fuels much of the anti-nuclear movement. Stanley Hauerwas has helpfully distinguished between "suvivalism" and Christian pacifism.[34] Christians are to break the hold of fear without losing their horror of nuclear evil. Hans Morgenthau commented that major nuclear war would destroy the meaning of life for those without transcendent faith. By robbing death of individuality and dignity it would destroy the meaning of death as well. Morgenthau wrote,

> The possibility of nuclear death, by destroying the meaning of life and death has reduced to absurd cliches the noble words of yesterday. To defend freedom and civilization is reduced to absurdity when to defend them amounts to destroying them.[35]

There is a truth to these words whether or not one has faith. Yet the final question of meaning lies beyond human grasp. Christians believe that the meaning of history was somehow, mysteriously revealed in the cross and the resurrection. Thus Paul could write.

> Death is swallowed up in victory. O death, where is thy victory? O death where is thy sting? The sting of death is sin, and the power of sin is the law. But thanks be to God, who gives us the victory through our Lord Jesus Christ.[36]

Christian faith in meaning beyond death is comprehensible only as it is expressed in the context of a person's life and social situation. What may be called "the way of the cross" cannot be adequately articulated in abstract terms that are separate from the life and "story" of an individual or community. Yoder writes,

> The question, Are Christian principles relevant to the social order? is misleading in its simplicity since it presupposes the permanent and objective element in ethical truth is a set of disincarnate principles so that these principles may be transposed from one frame of reference to another without further thought.[37]

The meaning of Christian ethics is not abstract but is tied to the life and history of the Christian community. The task of the Chruch, in relation to the bomb, is to be a community that expresses in its lifestyle the truth it has received. The nature of Christian ethics is expressed in the being of the Church as it responds to God and to the concrete historical/political events of its day. Dietrich Bonhoeffer asked,

> Who stands fast? Only the man whose final standard is not his reason, his principles, his conscience, his freedom or his virtue, but who is ready to sacrifice all this when he is called to obedient and responsible allegiance to God—the responsible man who tries to make his whole life an answer to the question and call of God.[38]

Ethical Policy Formation: from the Ideal to the Actual

The most significant problem for a Christian who seeks to influence policy formation is to relate Christian ideals to actual policy making. In political decision making the ideal can only take on real content through a series of intermediate steps. These steps may be thought of as graded "middle axioms" for the construction of policy.[39] Idealism is thwarted because it equates the ideal with the possible. Christian policy makers (or influencers) must distinguish between the actual, the possible, the desirable and the ideal. By doing so the ideal can reveal a direction for ethical policy analysis without being shipwrecked on the rocks of reality.

The Difference between Actual and Stated Policy

The actual defense policy of the United States is different from the stated defense policy for three main reasons. First there is a conscious difference based on deterrence strategy. In a war of nerves and threats, deterrence strategy is distinguished from war- fighting strategy. When risks are deterred with risks the trick is to convince the opponent of the reality of a risk while secretly keeping the risk as low as possible. A public threat may not be backed by a policy intended to carry it out. Apart from the obvious ethical problems of deception and secrecy there is the added problem of indeterminacy. Even those who consciously construct the gap between public and secret policy cannot be sure how close their actual behavior will conform to either, in a time of crisis. For the ethicist there is no choice but to evaluate the public policy and ignore what is not known.

Secondly, actual and stated policy differ from each other because of the self-deception or conscious hypocrisy of the leaders. Public defense policy is a tool of public relations and political propaganda. All recent American presidents have expressed a fervent desire to do away with nuclear weapons. Even if such expressions reflect a sincere hypothetical wish, it is heavily outweighed by other values.

Belligerent and warlike policy statements are just as prone to be motivated by propagandistic purposes. When the political mood of a nation turns "macho" the public statements of politicians tend to reflect public opinion. Ethical analysis can and should criticize the moral character of public policy statements, even if they are pure propaganda. People should be made aware of, for example, the fact that extreme scare stories about the Russians regularly come at budget making time. The actual policy of government is usually distinguishable from propaganda by acute political observers.

The third reason may be termed the efficiency gap. A large chasm may separate a stated policy from its implementation at the bureaucratic level. Political ethical analysis should consider both sides of the efficiency gap. Bureaucratic implementation of policy is both a technical and an ethical problem. Institutional momentum which thwarts individual policy decisions may point out the reign of "principalities and powers" that transcend human agency.[40]

All three reasons for the gap between stated and actual policy combine moral and technical problems. From a Christian perspective, evil is an objective reality in human affairs. Effective moral analysis needs technical and political skill to address both stated and actual policy. In the labryinth of international relations policy, many questions may be addressed by moralists before they are adequately understood.

The Probable Results of a Policy

Teleological reasoning demands calculation of the outcome of policy. The awesome proportions of a nuclear disaster lend urgency to the need for what amounts to prophecy. In 1964 two respected scientists, Jerome Wiesner and Herbert York came to the following grim conclusion:

Both sides in the arms race are thus confronted by the dilemma of steadily increasing military power and steadily decreasing national security. It is our considered professional judgement that this dilemma has no technical solution. If the great powers continue to look for solutions in the area of science and technology alone, the result will be to worsen the situation. The clearly predictable course of the arms race is a steady open spiral downward into oblivion.[41]

Political policy makers are usually forced by the pressures of the present to address short term problems. Sometimes even staunch supporters of current defense strategy concede that the long term possibilities of avoiding major nuclear war appear dim.[42] Yet, as Richard Falk observed, "It borders on the pathological to favor a course of action that we actively suppose will lead to... thermonuclear war.[43]

Current policy is not a static reality but a changing phenomenon. Many writers who accept the short term necessity of deterrence emphatically reject it as a permanent solution. In the short term, deterrence may prevent war. But in the long term deterrence means disaster. Thus Bishop Roger Mahony allows for a possible Catholic support of deterrence under three conditions:

First that the primary moral imperative is to prevent any use of nuclear weapons under any circumstances; second, that the possession of nuclear weapons is always an evil which could at best be tolerated, but only if the deterrence strategy is used in order to make progress on arms limitation and reduction; third, that the ultimate goal of what remains at best an interim policy is the eventual elimination of nuclear arms and of the threat of mutual assured destruction.[44]

Mahony concludes that present deterrence strategy does not meet any of these requirements and therefore should be resisted by Roman Catholics. Mahony's rejection of present deterrence policy is thus based on a judgment about the motivations of political policy, the purposes of the policy and the direction in which it is moving. Mahony's consideration of the long term direction of policy is a good illustration of how contingent political reasoning can operate with deontological limits.

Objections to deterrence are often met with a request for

politically viable alternatives.   There are many ways of calculating the politically possible.   On one level the politically possible simply depends on the will of those in power, their perception of the national interest and sufficient popular backing for them to remain in power long enough to implement a change in strategy.   From this perspective the implementation of an alternative, morally desirable defense policy depends on changing the opinions of policy makers and public opinion.

At a more substantive level politically possible policies are those which, if implemented, can bring about the goals for which they were designed.   From this perspective the politically possible depends upon the definition of reachable national goals.   The implementation of policies designed to reach such goals depends on the opinion and will of leaders and their constituency.

A third definition of the politically possible relies on the relations and interactions of all those who will put it into effect.   Thus a bilateral agreement to eliminate intermediate range missiles from Europe is only possible if both parties to it are willing and able to agree upon mutually acceptable conditions for the agreement.   Politically responsible ethical criticism faces the difficult task of proposing realistic alternatives that are potentially acceptable to all those who will carry them out.

Politically possible, or realistc policy goals are not necessarily likely.   Former Ambassador George F. Kennan suggested the radical idea that the United States propose to the Soviet government an immediate across-the-boards reduction, by 50 percent, of the nuclear arsenals now being maintained by the superpowers.   Given the right conditions and supported by sufficient public opinion Kennan's proposal could be considered politically realistic. It now appears far more realistic than when he proposed it.   Other possibilities include renewal of the ABM treaty, completion of a Test Ban treaty, agreement on "de-MIRVing" current missiles, making a "no first use" declaration, and halting research on the Strategic Defense Initiative.

Even if their specific form is not implemented in the near future, such proposals are not inherently unrealistic and they serve the political purpose of widening the policy options under public consideration. By doing so they help redefine the policy question in terms of how we can lessen the criminal burden of nuclear weapons.

Christian policy makers may sometimes support a policy that is politically realistic even though it is abhorent to them in the abstract. The basis on which a policy of finite deterrence may be politically supported by a pacifist Christian is twofold. First, it may be supported as a lesser evil to the current competition for supremacy.

Secondly, deterrence may be supported because it is required by the values of the nation. A politician has a responsibility, within limits, to support the values of his constituency. The limits include deontological principles as well as the politician's perception of contingent moral value. A policy maker may judge deterrence to be objectively the most moral and effective policy, given the presuppositions of pluralism. As a governmental "servant", the Christian politician should not treat policy as a means of imposing particular Christian values if they are clearly contradictory of the basic values of the nation. National security is part of the definition of a modern nation-state. A pacifist politician must consider what is the best, politically possible way for the state to protect the physical security of its people.[45]

Distinguishable from the politically possible is the politically desirable. The politically desirable is not pure utopianism in that it does not ignore the insecurities of international politics. The politically desirable assumes the highest possible political values of the nation from a Christian perspective. Such values are perhaps unlikely to ever be dominant in the United States and therefore the desirable cannot be considered realistic, or "possible."

A politically desirable defense policy might include bilateral, or failing that, a unilateral nuclear cutback to a very small nuclear deterrent arsenal. Major unilateral arms reduction would presuppose a drastic change in American national values. Such a cutback would be preceeded by lesser unilateral initiatives that used various incentives to encourage reciprocal cutbacks on the part of the Soviets. If bilateral arms reductions did not succeed, unilateral cutbacks would proceed. If bilateral arms reductions did succeed, negotiations for nuclear disarmament could follow.

A problem with some, ethical, anti-war proposals is that they mistake the politically desirable for the politically realistic. The sequence I have suggested shows the direction in which policy should head but also indicates the priorities for political action.

Beyond the politically desirable it is possible to postulate abstracted Christian political ideals that indicate the further direction of Christian political ideals. In the economic realm the "Jubilee principle" might be one such ideal.[46] In the area of defense policy, non-violent resistance might be another. The attempt by Charles Beitz to apply John Rawl's concept of "justice as fairness" to international relations is a third example.[47] Abstracted Christian political ideals correspond to the concept of "utopia" advocated by the Latin American theologian Gustavo Gutierrez.[48]

Utopia points to a direction, but unlike the sequence from the actual to the desirable, it is not reformist but revolutionary. Utopia is related to the historical by means of denunciation and annunciation. Christian political ideals reveal, by contrast with the actual, the moral bankruptcy of the present political, social and economic order. They also portray a different order of human relationship that is projected onto the future.

While Gutierrez sounds confident of the ultimate historical fulfillment of his utopia, I am not. Like Gutierrez I believe that authentic utopian thought must be related through praxis to the present. Christian political ideals illuminate a direction for governmental policy, but they serve a more direct function for the political direction of Christian individuals and communities. Christians are to incarnate political ideals of the Kingdom of God in their relations with each other and the world at large, even if they cannot impose them on government.

The political task of most Christians is not to formulate realistic defense policy but vigorously to resist the present nuclear policy. In political ethics the politics of protest is different from the politics of reform. Both are needed. But most Christians will not, and should not, attempt detailed policy formulation. Christians are not epistemologically situated in a better position than other people regarding how the burden of nuclear weapons may be lessened. Policy formulation requires expertise, not only concerning issues in the abstract, but of the shifting and subtle distinctions between the actual, the probable, the possible, the realistic and the desirable.

There are two basic reasons why Christians should resist and protest nuclear defense policy. The first reason is held in common by both Christians and non-Christians. Present nuclear policy should be protested because it violates many of the fundemental, professed values of our country. One need not be an ethicist to see that nuclear weapons are immoral. Rational deterrence was reached twenty-five years ago. The continued arms race is dangerous, unnecessary, costly foolish and immoral. On that basis anyone can and should be driven to protest.

The second basis for resistance to the arms race is unique to Christians. The primary calling of all Christians is to unveil the reality of the Kingdom of God that was revealed in Jesus Christ. United States nuclear policy massively violates the values of the Kingdom of God. As part of their witness to these values Christians are to reject complicity with evil. They are also called to expose it. Paul wrote to the Ephesians,

> Let no one deceive you with empty words... for once you were darkness, but now you are light in the Lord; walk as children of light... Take no part in the unfruitful works of darkness but instead expose them.[49]

Jesus was a master of the politics of protest. Everywhere he went he provoked confrontation with the political and religious leaders of his day. In his actions and in his speech he exposed the hypocricy and corruption of the elite.[50] With his quiet ability to draw large crowds and his fearless adherence to truth, it is not surprising that his public ministry only lasted three years before he was executed.

Nuclear weapons are an apt symbol of the power of death in our world. Protest and resistance against that power need not be politically effective in order to be significant. Protest as a form of witness to the Kingdom of God may be primarily motivated by a desire to speak the truth in love, whatever the consequences. This should not rule out protest as a political strategy nor encourage irresponsible protest. But there is an integrity to a voice raised in public protest as a witness to the truth. This integrity is not diminished if no one listens or cares. Nor is it invalidated by the lack of a rationally articulated alternative political policy. The politics of protest are different from the politics of reform.

A Christian politics of protest should be an integral part of the life of a community. There must be a lived out basis for protest. If protest is not a political strategy and not backed by realistic alternatives, then it must be based in a living community. If protest is simply based on idealism then it is not productive. The integrity of protest is based upon a concrete embodiment of the values the protester professes. Protest without a lived basis in alternative values is the result of either naivete or hypocricy. As Ronald Sider observed,

> Much recent Christian social action has been ineffective because Christian leaders called on the government to legislate what they could not persuade their church members to practice voluntarily.[51]

The Kingdom of God is a political reality that should be reflected in the life of a Christian community. Those who live with Christ as King must grapple with a new set of values that change all their relationships to the political, social and economic order. Stanley Hauerwas wrote,

> It is the duty of the Church to be a society which through the way its members deal with one another demonstrates to the world what love means in socal relations. So understood the Church fulfills its social responsibility by being an example, a witness, a creative minority formed by its obedience to non-resistant love.[52]

Two levels of action may be discerned for a politics of protest against nuclear defense policy. The first may be called the politics of personal refusal. At the personal level the most significant area is the choice of a profession. Defense related jobs and professions are creeping into more and more sectors of the economy. The Defense Department is one of the largest employers in the United States. Christians need to make the costly decision not to lend their professional lives to the futher development of the military-industrial-labor-academic complex.[53] Personal refusal may impinge on everything from lifestyle and economic value choices to draft resistance and tax resistance.

The second level of protest has been through public activities that range from the proposal of symbolic or substantive policy alternatives, to extreme acts of public civil disobedience such as breaking into nuclear weapons facilities and destroying nuclear warheads.[54] Public protest may be based on a strategy of political education or it may be motivated by a simple desire to witness to the truth before God and whoever else happens to listen. Perhaps the most effective recent form of public protest has been the dramatic and detailed letters of protest issued by members of the Roman Catholic hierarchy leading up to the Bishops' pastoral letter, The Challenge of Peace.[55]

The possibilities for both personal and public protest are endless. Protest requires hard work, careful thought and, for the Christian, prayer. Protest requires education. Well informed and thoughtful protest is relatively rare. But educated protest is vital to any political movement. Protest requires imagination. Most people are not initially reached by rational discourse but by powerful symbols that transcend the spoken word.

By far the most significant basis of protest for the Christian is love. When protest is motivated by fear and hate, or cynicsm and rebelliousness, it repels those who do not already agree. Christians are called to speak the truth in love, to listen to those who disagree and to sound an alarm to waken those who sleep in the face of grave peril.

There is an acute tension between Christian morality and nuclear policy. No single solution to that tension exists. As a Christian, an individual must absolutely reject the evil threat of defense by commitment to genocide. Yet as a citizen a Christian must also shoulder the criminal burden of our society's collective reliance on nuclear weapons. We must not tolerate the fact that our country's position of wealth and privilege in the world, along with some of our better values, are all defended by our willingness to threaten the world with an apocalypse.

Yet the requirements of political necessity offer no immediate solution to the nuclear problem. Nuclear weapons are permanent and intolerable, morally abhorrent and politically necessary. Thus we are left with a modest but formidable question: How can we reduce the criminal burden of the possession of nuclear weapons?

I have suggested two main answers. One is through the formation of actual political policy that moves in the direction of Christian ideals. Such policy can wean us from our nuclear addicition through politically feasible means. There are numerous political requirements for making this possible that we have not discussed. The most obvious of these is the continuing need to ease relations with the Soviet Union.

Christian ethics cannot be satisfied with the unending struggle to reform U.S. defense policy through governmental channels. In the face of the monumental threat that lies over the world and the scourge of global injustice that is perpetuated by arms spending, the Christian must take to the streets. Only the massive protest of people all over the world offers hope that the danger of holocaust may be abated.

1   Stanley Hoffmann, *Duties Beyond Borders* (Syracuse, NY: Syracuse University, 1981), pp. 83-84.

2   Stephen Neill, *The Interpretation of the New Testament* (London: Oxford University, 1964), p. 237.

3   Johathan Schell, *The Fate of the Earth* (New York: Alfred A. Knopf, 1982), pp. 181-231.

4   Even tax resistors pay for nuclear weapons in the sense that the common resources of the nation are spent on nuclear weapons. I mean to imply that on a deeper level than economics, nuclear weapons are the offspring of our common culture. We share a "corporate guilt."

5   This breakdown of figures is quoted in Roger Mahony "Becoming a Church of Peace Advocacy," *Christianity and Crisis*, 42, No. 3 (March 1, 1982): 41. Ten hours is about 600 million. At least six million die every year of malnutrition.

6   Erich Fromm, "Explorations into the Unilateral Disarmament Position," in John C. Bennett, ed., *Nuclear Weapons and the Conflict of Conscience* (New York: Charles Scribner's Sons, 1962), p. 130.

7   John C. Bennett, "Moral Urgencies in the Nuclear Context," ibid., p. 101.

8   Michael Walzer, *Just and Unjust Wars* (New York: Basic Books, 1977), p. 271.

9   The economics of military spending cannot be really measured either. It is often argued that defense spending is non-productive and fuels both inflation and unemployment.

10   Roger Shinn, "A Dilemma, Seen from Several Sides," *Christianity and Crisis*, 41, No. 22 (Jan. 18, 1982): 375.

11   Augustine, in Joan, Ep. XXIV, 10, Mique Pl. XXXV paraphrased by Roland Bainton, *Christian Attitudes to War and Peace* (Nashville: Abingdon, 1960), p. 91.

12   Augustine, *The City of God*, Bk. XIX, Ch. 12.

13   The elitism of some within the scientific/military community cannot be sustained. Reagan Advisor Edward Teller recently pontificated, "Our policy of military secrecy is very badly overdone. It makes the public discussion irrational because it wipes out the difference between people who know what they are talking about and those who do not. Those who do know are not allowed to say what they know. Therefore the whole discussion is made on an uninformed basis." in "For and Against a Freeze," *Time*

14   Reinhold Niebuhr, *The Children of Light and the Children of Darkness* (New York: Charles Scribner's Sons, 1944), p. 118.

15 A classic typology of the different approaches is contained in H. Richard Niebuhr's *Christ and Culture* (New York: Harper and Brothers, 1956).

16 John Howard Yoder, *The Christian Witness to the State* (Newton, Kansas: Faith and Life Press, 1964), p. 7.

17 Ibid., p. 23.

18 Ibid., p. 33.

19 Reinhold Niebuhr, *Christianity and Power Politics* (New York: Charles Scribner's Sons, 1940), p. 14.

20 Reinhold Niebuhr, *The Children of Light*, p. 73.

21 Reinhold Niebuhr, *Moral Man and Immoral Society* (New York: Charles Scribner's Sons, 1932), p. 71.

22 Reported by Ronald J. Sider of a statement the President made during a White House breakfast with Evangelical leaders in January, 1980. The incident is cited in Ronald J. Sider and Richard Taylor, *Nuclear Holocaust and Christian Hope* (Downers Grove, IL: InterVarsity/Paulist, 1982)

23 Richard A. Falk, *Law, Morality and War in the Contemporary World* (New York: Frederick A. Praeger, 1963), p. 6.

24 John C. Bennett, *Christian Realism* (New York: Charles Scribner's Sons, 1947), pp. 108ff.

25 José Míguez Bonino says "...there is no truth outside or beyond the concrete historical events in which men are involved as agents. There is, therefore, no knowledge except in action itself, in the process of transformimg the world through participation in history." *Doing Theology in a Revolutionary Situation* (Philadelphia: Fortress, 1975), p. 88. This is more than I want to say. All language abstracts from events and action is just as ambiguous as language. However, the relation between truth and action is closer than most writer and talkers are willing to admit.

26 E.g. Gordon Zahn, "A Religious Pacifist Look at Abortion," *Commonweal*, 94 (May 28, 1971) : 282.

27 Luke 12:22ff; Matthew 5:38-48; Mark 8:34-37. RSV used in all Biblical quotations.

28 John Howard Yoder, *The Original Revolution* (Scottdale, PA: Herald, 1971), p. 29.

29 Matthew 6:19-21.

30 Luke 12:29-31.

31 Mark 10:42-45.

32 Isaiah 31:1-3 cf. 30:15-17.

33 John Howard Yoder, *The Original Revolution*, p. 38.

34 Stanley Hauerwas, "Against the Nations: War and Survival in a Liberal Society" (Minneapolis: Winston Press, 1985).

35   Hans Morgenthau, "Death in the Nuclear Age" *Commentary,* September, 1961.

36   I Corinthians 15:54-57.

37   John Howard Yoder, *The Christian Witness to the State,* p. 29.

38   Dietrich Bonhoeffer, *Letters and Papers from Prison,* Eberhard Bethage, ed. (New York: Macmillan, 1972), p. 5.

39   See John C. Bennett, *Christian Ethics and Social Policy* (New York: Charles Scribner's Sons, 1946), pp. 76ff. The term "middle axioms" was first used by J.H. Oldham in W.A. Visser t'Hooft and J.H. Oldham, The Church and its Function in Society (Chicago: Willett, Clarck, 1937), pp. 193ff.

40   This is the assertion of William Stringellow, *An Ethic for Christians and Other Aliens in A Strange Land* (Waco, TX: Word Book, 1973). See especially Chapter Three, "The Moral Reality Named Death." A similar thesis is advanced by Jacques Ellul in all his books, especially, *The Political Illusion* (New York: Vintage Books, 1967) and *The Technological Society* (New York: Vintage Books, 1964).

41   Jerome Wiesner and Herbert York "The Test Ban," *Scientific American,* October, 1964, p. 35.

42   cf. Oskar Morgenstern, *The Question of National Defense* (New York: Random House, 1961), p. 326.

43   Richard A. Falk, *Law, Morality and War* p. 50.

44   Roger Mahony, "Becoming a Church of Peace Advocacy," p. 38.

45   George Kaufman makes a similar point. His emphasis is on acceptance of the neighbor with whom one disagrees. Kaufman suggests that as pacifists we ought to be prepared, "along with our negative witness, to support the military bill most in accord with the highest ideals and best insights of the total American society," in "Non-Resistance and Responsibility," *Concern,* No. 6 (November, 1958), p. 16.

46   See Exodus 25. Cf. John Howard Yoder, *The Politics of Jesus* (Grand Rapids, Michigan: Wm. B. Eerdmans, 1972), pp. 64-77.

47   Charles R. Beitz, *Political Theory and International Relations* (Princeton, NJ: Princeton University Press, 1979), pp. 125- 183. Beitz mistakes his political ideals for potentially realistic policy. By doing so he underestimates the structural pressures in international relations and the falleness of human nature.

48   Gustavo Gutierrez, *A Theology of Liberation* (Maryknoll, NY: Orbis, 1973), pp. 232-239.

49   Ephesians 5:5,8 & 11.

50   See for example Luke 11:37-54.

51   Ronald J. Sider, *Rich Christians in an Age of Hunger* (Downers Grove, IL: Inter-Varsity, 1977), p. 205.

52 Stanley Hauerwas, *Vision and Virtue: Essays in Christian Ethical Reflection* (Notre Dame, Ind.: Fides, 1974), pp. 211-212.
53 A dramatic example of the politics of personal refusal was provided recently by Bishop LeRoy Matthiesen of Amarillo, Texas. Bishop Matthiesen called on all Catholics who worked at a large local weapons plant to resign on the basis of conscience. Subsequently he set up a fund to provide economic assistance to all those who followed his advice.
54 After Daniel Berrigan broke into the Pantex weapons plant and hammered on some Mark 12A warheads, he ironically called it the first act of nuclear disarmament in the history of the world!
55 National Conference of Catholic Bishops, *"The Challenge of Peace: God's Promise and our Response"* (Washington, D.C.: U.S. Catholic Conference, 1983).

SELECTED BIBLIOGRAPHY

Aldridge, Robert C., *The Counterforce Syndrome*. 2nd ed. Washington, D.C. : Institute for Policy Studies, 1979.

Anscombe, Elizabeth, "War and Murder." In *War and Morality*, pp.42-53, edited by Richard A. Wasserstrom. Belmont, CA: Wadsworth, 1970.

Aspin, Les, "What Are the Russians Up To?" *International Security* 3, No. 1 (Summer 1978): 30-54.

Augustine, *The City of God*. Translated by Marcus Dods. Great Books of the Western World, Vol. 18. Chicago: Encyclopedia Britannica, 1957.

Aukerman, Dale, *Darkening Valley*. New York: Seabury, 1981.

Bainton, Roland H., *Christian Attitudes to War and Peace*. Nashville: Abingdon, 1960.

Beitz, Charles R., *Political Theory and International Relations*. Princeton, NJ: Princeton University Press, 1979.

Bennett, John C., *Christian Ethics and Social Policy*. New York: Charles Scribner's Sons, 1946.

Bennett, John C., "Countering the Theory of Limited Nuclear War." *The Christian Century*, January 7-14, 1981, pp. 10-13.

Bennett, John C., ed., *Nuclear Weapons and the Conflict of Conscience*. New York: Charles Scribner's Sons, 1962.

"Soviet Arms and Priorities: The Need for a New Debate." *Christianity and Crisis* 41, No. 15 (October 19, 1981): 275-279.

Bennett, John C. and Seifert, Harvey, *U.S. Foreign Policy and Christian Ethics*. Philadelphia: Westminster, 1977.

Bonhoeffer, Dietrich, *Letters and Papers from Prison*. The Enlarged Edition, edited by Eberhard Bethage. New York: Macmillan Publishing Co., 1953.

Bonkovsky, Frederick O., *International Norms and National Policy*. Grand Rapids, Mich: Wm. B. Eerdmans, 1980.

Brodie, Bernard, ed., *The Absolute Weapon: Atomic Power and World Order*. New York: Harcourt Brace, 1946.

Brown, Harold, *Annual Department of Defense Report, Fiscal Year 1981*. Washington D.C. : Government Printing Office, 1981.

Brown, Harold O.J., "Rumors of War." *Eternity*, June, 1980. pp. 16-17.

Bundy, McGeorge; Kennan, G.F.; McNamara, R.; and Smith, G, "Nuclear Weapons and the Atlantic Alliance." *Foreign AFfairs* 60, No. 4 (Spring 1982): 753-768.

Burt, Richard, "Reassessing the Strategic Balance." *International Security* 5, No. 1 (Summer 1980).

Camus, Albert, *Neither Victims Nor Executioners.* New York: Continuum, 1980.

Carr, Edward Hallett, *The Twenty Years Crisis, 1919-1939: An Introduction to the Study of International Relations.* New York: Harper and Row, 1964.

Cesaretti, C.A. and Vitale, Joseph T., *Rumors of War.* New York: Seabury, 1982.

Chapman, G. Clarke, *Facing the Nuclear Heresy.* Elgin, IL: Brethern, 1986.

Chernus, Ira, *"Mythologies of Nuclear War."* Paper presented at the American Academy of Religion Annual Meeting, San Francisco, CA, December 19-21, 1981.

Childress, James F, "Just War Criteria." In *War or Peace: The Search for New Answers,* pp. 40-58, edited by Thomas A. Shannon, Maryknoll, NY : Orbis, 1981.

Cicero, Marcus Tullius, *De Officiis/On Duties.* Translated by Harry G. Edinger. New York: Bobbs-Merrill Co., 1974.

Clausewitz, Carl Von, *On War.* Edited and translated by Michael Howard and Peter Paret. Princeton, NJ: Princeton University Press, 1976.

Clouse, Robert G., editor, *War: Four Christian Views.* Downers Grove, IL: InterVarsity, 1981.

Combes, Gustave, *La Doctrine Politique de Saint Augustin.* Paris, 1927.

Dorn, Walter. "European Militarism." In *A History of Military Affairs,* edited by Gordon B. Turner. New York: Harcourt Brace, 1952.

Dougherty, James E. and Pflatzgraff, Robert L., *Contending Theories of International Relations.* New York: J.B. Lippincott, 1971.

Douglass, James, *The Non-Violent Cross.* New York: Macmillan, 1966.

Drinan, Robert, "Is Pacifism the Only Option Left for Christians?" In *War and Christian Ethics,* edited by Arthur F. Holmes. Grand Rapids, Mich.: Baker Book House, 1975.

Dunn, Lewis A., *Controlling the Bomb.* New Haven: Yale

University Press, 1982.

Earle, Edward Meade, "The Influence of Air Power on History." In *A History of Military Affairs.*, edited by Gordon B. Turner. New York: Harcourt Brace, 1952.

Eisenhower, Dwight D., *Mandate for Change, 1953-1956.* New York: Doubleday, 1963.

Eller, Vernard, *War and Peace from Genesis to Revelation.* Scottdale, PA: Herald, 1981.

Ellsberg, Daniel, *Nuclear Armament.* Berkeley, CA: Conservation Press, 1980.

Ellul, Jacques, *The Political Illusion.* New York: Vintage Books, 1967.

Enthoven, Alain, "1963 Nuclear Strategy Revisited." In *Ethics and Nuclear Strategy*, edited by Harold P. Ford and Francis X. Winters, S.J. Maryknoll, NY: Orbis, 1977.

Enthoven, Alain and Smith, K. Wayne, *How Much Is Enough?* New York: Harper and Row, 1971.

Falk, Richard A., *Law, Morality and War in the Contemporary World.* New York: Frederick A. Praeger, 1963.

Ford, John C., "The Morality of Obliteration Bombing." *Theological Studies* 5, 1944.

Ford, Harold P. and Winters, Francis X., eds., *Ethics and Nuclear Strategy?* Maryknoll, NY: Orbis, 1977.

Frankena, William K., *Ethics.* 2nd ed. Englewood Cliffs, NJ: Prentice-Hall, 1973.

Freedman, Lawrence, *The Evolution of Nuclear Strategy.* New York: St. Martin's, 1981.

Fromm, Erich, "Explorations into the Unilateral Disarmament Position." In *Nuclear Weapons and the Conflict of Conscccience,* edited by John C. Bennett. New York: Charles Scribner's Sons, 1962.

Gardiner, Robert, *The Cool Arm of Destruction.* Philadelphia: Westminister, 1974.

George, Alexander L. and Smoke, Richard, *Deterrence in American Foreign Policy.* New York: Columbia University Press, 1974.

Gessert, Robert and Hehir, J. Bryan, *The New Nuclear Debate.* New York: Council on Religion and International Affairs, 1976.

Geyer, Alan, *The Idea of Disarmament,* Second Edition. Elgin, IL: Brethren, 1982.

Goodwin, Geoffrey, *Ethics and Nuclear Deterrence.* New York: St. Martin's Press, 1982.

Gray, Colin S., "Action and Reaction in the Nuclear Arms Race." *Military Review* 51 (August 1971): 16-26.

Greenwood, Ted, *Making the MIRV: A Study of Defense Decision Making.* Cambridge, MA: Ballinger, 1975.

Grinspoon, Lester, editor, *The Long Darkness.* New Haven: Yale University Press, 1986.

Gutierrez, Gustavo, *A Theology of Liberation.* Maryknoll, NY: Orbis, 1973.

Haas, Ernst B., "The Balance of Power: Prescription, Concept or Propaganda?" *World Politics* V (July 1953): 442-477.

Haas, Ernst B.,*Beyond the Nation-State.* Stanford, CA: Stanford, 1964.

Haldeman, Harry R. with Di Mona, Joseph, *The Ends of Power.* New York: Times Books, 1978.

Harvard Nuclear Study Group, *Living With Nuclear Weapons,* New York: Bantam, 1983.

Hatfield, (Senator) Mark O., "The Age of Anxiety: Emerging Nuclear Tensions in the 1980's." *Report for Senator Hatfield*, No. 193. Washington, D.C., June, 1981.

Hauerwas, Stanley, *Against the Nations: War and Survival in a Liberal Society.* Minneapolis: Winston, 1983.

Hegel, G.W.F., *Philosophy of Right.* Oxford: Clarendon, 1942.

Hehir, J. Bryan, "The Just War Ethic and Catholic Theology." In *War or Peace? The Search for New Answers.* edited by Thomas A. Shannon. Maryknoll, NY: Orbis, 1980.

Herz, John H., *International Politics in the Atomic Age.* New York: Columbia University Press, 1959.

Heyer, Robert, *Nuclear Disarmament: Key Statements of Popes, Bishops, Councils and Churches.* New York: Paulist, 1982.

Hobbes, Thomas, *Leviathan.* edited by Nelle Fuller. The Great Books vol. 23. Chicago: Encyclopedia Britannica, 1952.

Hoffman, Stanley, *Duties Beyond Borders.* New York: Syracuse University Press, 1981.

Hollenbach, S.J., David, *Nuclear Ethics.* New York: Paulist, 1983.

Holloway, David, *The Soviet Union and the Arms Race.* New Haven: Yale University Press, 1983.

Holmes, Arthur F., ed., *War and Christian Ethics*. Grand Rapids, MI: Baker Book House, 1975.

Hume, David, *Essays and Treatises on Several Subjects*. Edinburgh: Bell and Bradfute and W. Blackwood, 1825. Reprinted in *World Politics*. edited by Arend Lyphart. Boston: Allyn & Bacon, 1966.

Humphrey, Hubert H. "The State of the Question, An Introduction." in *ABM: Yes or No?* Center for the Study of Democratic Institutions. Santa Barabara, CA: Fund for the Republic, 1969.

Huntington, Samuel P., "Arms Races: Prerequisites and Results." *Public Policy* 8 (1958): 41-86.

Huntington, Samuel P., ed., *Changing Patterns of Military Politics*. New York: Free Press of Glencoe, 1962.

Jervis, Robert, "Why Nuclear Superiority Doesn'tMatter." *Political Science Quarterly* 94 (Winter 1979-1980).

Johnson, James Turner, *Ideology, Reason, and the Limitation of War*. Princeton, NJ: Princeton University, 1975.

Kahn, Gerome H., *Security In the Nuclear Age*. Washington, D.C.: The Brookings Institute, 1975.

Kaufman, Gordon, "Non-Resistance and Responsibility." *Concern* No. 6. (November 1958).

Kennan, George F., "U.S.-Soviet Relations: Turning from Catastrophe." *Christianity and Crisis* 40, No. 9. (May 26, 1980): 155-158.

Keohane, Robert and Nye, Joseph. *Power and Interdependence*. New York: Little, Brown and Co., 1977.

Klassen, William, *Love of Enemies: The Way to Peace*, Philadelphia: Fortress Press, 1984.

Kraybill, Donald B., *Facing Nuclear War*. New York: Crossroad, 1983.

Laarman, Edward J., *Nuclear Pacafism*, New York: Peter Lang, 1984.
Lasserre, Jean, *War and the Gospel*. Scottdale, PA: Herald, 1962.

Lasswell, Harold D., "The Garrison State Hypothesis Today" in *Changing Patterns of Military Politics*. edited by Samuel P. Huntington. New York: Free Press of Glencoe, 1962.

Lens, Sidney, *The Day Before Doomsday*. Boston: Beacon, 1977.

Levi, Werner, "The Relative Irrelevance of Moral Norms in International Relations." in *International Politics and Foreign Policy*.

edited by J. Rosenau. New York: Free, 1961.

Lifton, Robert J., *The Broken Connection.* New York: Simon and Schuster, 1979.

Machiavelli, Niccolo, *The Prince.* Translated by W.K. Marriot. *The Great Books,* vol. 23. Chicago: Encyclopedia Britannica, 1953.

Mahony, Bishop Roger, "Becoming a Church of Peace Advocacy." *Christianity and Crisis* 42, No.3. (March 1, 1982).

Mandelbaum, Michael, *The Nuclear Question.* New York: Cambridge University, 1979.

Martin, David and Mullen, Peter, *Unholy Warfare.* New York: Basil Blackwell, 1983.

Matheson, Peter, *A Just Peace.* New York: Friendship, 1981.

McSorley, Richard, *New Testament Basis of Peace Making.* Scottdale, PA: Herald Press, 1979.

Meadows, Donella H.; Meadows, D.L.; Randers, J.; and Behrens III, W.W., *The Limits to Growth.* New York: Signet, 1972.

Meinecke, Friedrich, *Machiavellism.* New Haven: Yale University Press, 1957.

Merton, Thomas, *On Peace.* New York: McCall, 1971.

Míguez Bonino, José, *Doing Theology in a Revolutionary Situation.* Philadelphia: Fortress, 1975.

Miller, Steven E. and Van Evera, Stephen, Editors, *The Star Wars Controversy.* Princeton: Princeton University, 1986.

Modelski, George, "Kautilya: Foreign Policy and International System in the Ancient Hindu World." *American Political Science Review* LVIII (September 1964): 549-560.

Morgenstern, Oskar, *The Question of National Defense.* New York: Random House, 1961.

Morgenthau, Hans, "Death in the Nuclear Age." *Commentary.* September 1961. New York: Alfred A. Knopf, 1951. Alfred A. Knopf, 1967.

Moss, Norman, *Men Who Play God.* New York: Harper and Row, 1968.

Murnion, Philip J., editor. *Catholics and Nuclear War.* New York: Crossroad, 1983.

Murray, John Courtney, "Remarks on the Moral Problem of War." *Theological Studies* XX, No. 1 (March 1959).

Myrdal, Alva, *The Game of Disarmament.* New York: Pantheon, 1976.

National Conference of Catholic Bishops, *The Challenge of Peace: God's Promise and Our Response.* Washington, D.C.: U.S. Catholic Conference, 1983.

Nye, Joseph S., *Nuclear Ethics.* New York: Free Press, 1986.

Peterson, Jeannie, *The Aftermath.* New York: Pantheon, 1983.

Rapoport, Anatol, *Conflict in a Man-Made Environment.* Baltimore: Penguin Books, 1974.

Rosencrance, Richard N., *Action and Reaction in World Politics.* Boston: Little, Brown and Co., 1963.

Rosenau, James N., ed., *International Politics and Foreign Policy.* New York: Free Press, 1961.

Rousseau, Jean-Jacques, *A Lasting Peace through the Federation of Europe and The State of War.* Translated by C.E. Vaughan. London: Constable, 1917.

Ruede, Ernest, *The Morality of War.* Rome: Pontifica Universitas Lateranensis, 1970.

Scheer, Robert, *With Enough Shovels: Reagan, Bush and Nuclear War.* New York: Vintage, 1983.

Schell, Jonathan, *The Fate of the Earth.* New York: Alfred A. Knopf, 1982.

Schelling, Thomas C. *Arms and Influence.* New Haven: Yale University Press, 1966.

Shannon, Thomas A., ed., *War or Peace? The Search for New Answers.* Maryknoll, NY: Orbis, 1980.

Shinn, Roger, "A Dilemma Seen from Several Sides." *Christianity and Crisis* 41, No. 22 (January 18, 1982).

Sider, Ronald J., *Rich Christians in an Age of Hunger.* Downers Grove, IL: InterVarsity, 1977.

Sider, Ronald J. and Taylor, Richard, *Nuclear Holocaust and Christian Hope.* Downers Grove, IL: InterVarsity, 1982.

Snow, Michael, *Christian Pacifism: Fruit of the Narrow Way.* Richmond, IN: Friends United, 1981.

Snyder, G.H., *Deterrence and Defense: Toward a Theory of National Security.* Princeton, NJ: Princeton University Press, 1961.

Soelle, Dorothy, *The Arms Race Kills, Even Without War.* Philadelphia: Fortress, 1983.

Spaeth, Robert, *No Easy Answers.* Minneapolis: Winston Press, 1983.

Stebbins, Richard, ed., *Documents and American Foreign Relations, 1962.* New York: Harper and Row, 1963.

Steinbrunner, John, "Beyond Rational Deterrence: The Struggle for New Conceptions," *World Politics* 28, No. 2 (January 1976).

Stringfellow, William, *An Ethic for Christians and Other Aliens in a Strange Land.* Waco, TX: Word Books, 1973.

Thompson, Kenneth W, "The Nuclear Dilemma—a Discussion." *Christianity and Crisis* XXI, No. 19 (November 13, 1961): 200- 204.

Thucydides, *The Peleponnesian War.* Translated by Rex Warner. Harmondsworth, IN: Penguin Books, 1954.

U.S. Arms Control Agency, *Worldwide Effects of Nuclear War: Some Perspectives. Report No. 81.* Washington D.C.: U.S. Government Printing Office, 1975.

U.S. Congress. Senate. Committee on Banking, Housing and Urban Affairs, *Economic and Social Consequences of Nuclear Attacks on the United States. A study prepared for the Joint Committee on Defense Production.* 96th Congress, 1st Session. Washington D.C.: U.S. Government Printing Office, 1979.

U.S. Congress. Senate. Office of Technology Assessment, *The Effects of Nuclear War. A study prepared for the Senate Committee on Foreign Relations.* Washington D.C.: U.S. Government Printing Office, 1980.

Visser t'Hooft, W.A. and Oldham, J.H., *The Church and its Function in Society.* Chicago: Willett, Clark, 1937.

Wadsworth, James, "Counterforce." *The Saturday Review,* July 28, 1962.

Walters, LeRoy B., Jr., *"Five Classic Just War Theories: A Study in the Thought of Thomas Aquinas, Vittoria, Suarez, Gentili and Grotius."* Ph.D. dissertation, Yale University, 1971.

Waltz, Kenneth N. *Man, the State, and War.* New York: Columbia University Press, 1954.

Walzer, Michael. *Just and Unjust Wars.* New York: Basic Books, 1977.

"Moral Judgement in Time of War." *In War and Morality,* edited by Richard A. Wasserstrom. Belmont, CA: Wadsworth, 1970.

Weisner, Jerome and York, Herbert. "The Test Ban." *Scientific American* (October 1964): 35.

Winters, Francis X. "The Bow or the Cloud." *America,* July 25, 1981.

Wohlstetter, Albert. "Is There a Strategic Arms Race?" *Foreign Policy* 15 (Summer 1974).

World Council of Churches study document. *"Christians and the Prevention of War in the Atomic Age."* No. 65. New York: World Council of Churches, 1958.

Wright, Quincy. *The Study of International Relations.* New York: Appleton-Century-Crofts, 1955.

Yoder, John Howard. *The Christian Witness to the State.* Newton, KS: Faith and Life, 1964.

Zahn, Gordon, "A Religious Pacifist Looks at Abortion." *Commonweal* 94 (May 28, 1971).

INDEX